Model United Nations
Unexpected Journey
Korea's Model UN Handbook

John Sang-Yup Lee

Model United Nations
Unexpected Journey
Korea's Model UN Handbook

John Sang-Yup Lee

한국문화사

To the Lord who brought miracles into my life
To my parents who allowed me to receive them

Copyright © 2015 by John Sang-Yup Lee
All rights reserved.
Every effort has been made to contact copyright holders and to obtain their permission for the use of all copyright material. If you believe that your copyright has been infringed please email john7454@naver.com with the relevant details.

Model United Nations:
Unexpected Journey Korea's Model UN Handbook

1판 1쇄 발행   2015년 12월 15일
1판 2쇄 발행   2020년 12월 30일

지 은 이 | 이상엽
펴 낸 이 | 김진수
펴 낸 곳 | 한국문화사
등   록 | 제1994-9호
주   소 | 서울특별시 성동구 아차산로49, 서울숲코오롱디지털타워3차, 404호
전   화 | 02-464-7708
팩   스 | 02-499-0846
이 메 일 | hkm7708@hanmail.net
홈페이지 | http://hph.co.kr

ISBN 978-89-6817-311-0 03740

• 이 책의 내용은 저작권법에 따라 보호받고 있습니다.
• 잘못된 책은 구매처에서 바꾸어 드립니다.
• 책값은 뒤표지에 있습니다.

• 이 도서의 국립중앙도서관 출판예정도서목록(CIP)은 서지정보유통지원시스템 홈페이지(http://seoji.nl.go.kr)와 국가자료공동목록시스템(http://www.nl.go.kr/kolisnet)에서 이용하실 수 있습니다.(CIP제어번호: CIP2015033723)

Acknowledgements

Best Delegate Institute	Chaehun Jung	Danny Hong
Eugine Choo	Ga Yeon Moon	Gayoon Lee
Hosung Ahn	Jeong ho Choi	Jihyun Lee
Jimin Kim	Jimin Jeong	Jion Jeong
Jiwoo Kim	Ji Yeon Rho	Jong Lim
Kevin Felix Chan	KMUN 2014	MaryAnn Shim
MIMUN 2012	Min Seok Park	Nayun Kim
Rinchong Kim	Sang Yoon Lee	Serim Jang
Seung Jae Hong	SIGMUN 2015	Tae Ho Park
Yeongshik Song	Yeonwoo Koo	

I especially appreciate Dr. Jin Park, Dr. Jaeho Hwang and Mr. Eric Moberg for their recommendations for this book; Professor Brandon Walcutt for his valuable feedback.

My special thanks go to Pastor Jinseok Nam, Chairman of the Board; Dr. In Chin Cho, Principal; Mr. Jong Myung Park, Homeroom teacher; and Pastor Byung Ik Jin, Director of Lydia Dormitory in GVCS for their heartfelt guidance.

I sincerely appreciate Pastor Hyun Sam Cho and Pastor Hyung Jun Lee in Seoul Light & Salt Church for their spiritual guidance.

I give my deepest appreciation to my well-beloved parents for helping me gain the experience to make this book and for helping me publish it.

※ All profits will be donated for the development of Korea's Model UN society

Letter of Recommendation 1

Dr. Jin Park
Chairman, Harvard Club of Korea
Former Chairman, Foreign Affairs, Trade and National Unification Committee
of the National Assembly (2008-2010)
Former Member, the 16th, 17th, 18th National Assembly of
the Republic of Korea (2002-2012)

John is one of Korea's prospective global leaders of the 21st century. He has achieved exceptional accomplishment of participating in more than twenty Model UN conferences, twice as a chair and many times as a delegate. Through his outstanding leadership as a vice-chair, John also contributed to the 2015 Harvard World Model UN conference held at Korea's KINTEX Convention Center. The book he wrote on the Model UN is one that every student interested in the Model UN should read as it is the best guidebook on the subject in Korea. It talks about the Model UN's Rules of Procedures, how to make speeches, how to make position papers, etc. Other than the Model UN, John has participated in various activities including youth committees, Taekwondo activities, and volunteer works through the UN's international youth initiatives, and was spotlighted for his remarkable leadership. The Republic of Korea is a country that was born as the only legitimate government on the Korean peninsula through the UN. It is also the country that blocked the communist tide to protect freedom and peace throughout the UN and the first Asian country to have one of its citizens become the Secretary General of the UN. I hope that John, like Ban Ki-moon, the UN Secretary General, act toward Korea's development and for the enhancement of international peace and security.

박진
하버드대학교 한국 총동문회장
전 국회외교통상통일 위원장 (2008-2010)
전 국회의원 (16, 17, 18대: 2002-2012)

　이상엽 군은 21세기에 장래가 촉망되는 한국의 글로벌 인재이다. 이군은 모의유엔 (Model UN) 대회를 20차례이상 치른 남다른 경험을 가지고 있다. 더구나 두 차례 걸쳐 의장으로 활동하였고, 대사로도 활동하였다. 얼마 전에 우리나라 일산 고양시에서 열렸던 2015 세계 모의유엔 대회에서는 부의장으로 탁월한 리더십을 발휘하여 행사를 성공적으로 치르는 데 크게 기여하였다. 이군이 저술한 책자는 모의유엔에 관심을 가지고 있는 학생이라면 반드시 읽어봐야 할 필독서다. 유엔 회의의 규정, 절차, 스피치 하는 법, 입장 표명, 연구 등 유엔 활동의 중요부분이 총망라 되어 있어서 세계모의유엔을 소개하는 최고의 길라잡이 가이드북이라고 볼 수 있다. 이군은 그 밖에도 청소년위원회 활동, 기자단 활동, 태권도 활동, 자원봉사 활동 등을 통해서 유엔을 통한 세계 청소년 공동체에서 뛰어난 리더십을 아낌없이 발휘하여 커다란 주목을 받았다. 대한민국은 유엔을 통하여 한반도의 유일한 합법정부로 태어났고, 유엔을 통하여 공산침략을 막고 자유와 평화를 지켰으며, 아시아에서 중국, 일본에 앞서 유엔사무총장을 배출한 나라다. 앞으로 이군이 반기문 유엔사무총장처럼 국제무대에서 대한민국의 발전과 세계평화 및 번영을 위해 눈부신 활약을 하게 될 날이 오기를 기대해본다.

Letter of Recommendation 2

Dr. Jaeho Hwang
Dean, External Relations & International Studies (한국외국어대 국제교류 · 대외협력처장)
Professor, Division of International Studies (한국외국어대 국제학부 교수)
at Hankuk University of Foreign Studies

Greeting very politely to me with wearing small glasses, that was my first impression on John Sang-yup Lee. He brought me about a 100-page book, who was known to me as just a high school student. I had this surprising feelings going on and on in my mind as I go through this book. Everything was written in English with very flowing and skillful writing techniques. It was hard to believe that it was written by a high school student because of his keen observation and unbelievable spectacular analyzing ability.

The book exposed well about Korean model as it introduces the concept of MUN. This would have been almost impossible if it were not been for his active participations and experiences of last four years. It was definitely the academic fruition proving that he never had neglected his school days.

As the writer mentioned in the preface of the book, everyone who read this book will have 'Unexpected Journey to Model UN,' as the title of the book. Through this, they will have 'a productive experience that allows (readers) to develop vital skills for their future.'

Letter of Recommendation 3

Mr. Eric Moberg
Debate/Model UN Teacher at Hankuk Academy of Foreign Studies
(용인한국외대부설고 토론/모의유엔 교사)

This book is comprehensive in its overview of Model United Nations in Korea including valuable sections on different styles and procedures as well as detailed advice for new delegates. I have participated in MUN for eight years in high school and university and for eight more years as a club advisor. Speaking from this experience, I know that Model UN: Unexpected Journey would be an outstanding resource for any Korean student starting out in this valuable activity.

The author speaks from his own extensive experience, including all roles at MUN conferences. Sections introducing and providing accurate examples for every aspect from writing position papers and resolutions to becoming an effective speaker in committee provide a step by step path for a new delegate to get the most from MUN.

After reading this book, I hope that students will gain as much as I have from MUN by developing skills in research, persuasion, public speaking, compromise, and forming new relationships.

Table of Contents

Acknowledgements vii
Letters of Recommendation viii

Preface 1

Chapter 1 What is Model United Nations? 4
   1.1. THIMUN Rules of Procedures in Korea 5
   1.2. UNA-USA Rules of Procedures in Korea 22

Chapter 2 Model UN of Korea 36
   2.1. Routes of Participation 37
   2.2. Various Domestic Conferences 57
   2.3. Market Trends 76

Chapter 3 Diverse Roles, Diverse Experiences 79
   3.1. Secretariat 80
   3.2. Student Officer 95
   3.3. Staff 104
   3.4. Delegate 107

Chapter 4 How to Be a 'Best Delegate' ········ 111
   4.1. Research, Research, and Research ········ 113
   4.2. Passion Shown through Speech and Performance ······ 118
   4.3. Model UNITED Nations ········ 121
   4.4. Position Paper, Resolution, Amendment ········ 124
   4.5. Special Tips & Advice ········ 142
   4.6. Award Selections ········ 151

Chapter 5 Post Model UN Activities ········ 156
   5.1. Youth Committees ········ 157
   5.2. International Events ········ 159
   5.3. Academics ········ 160
   5.4. Summer Programs ········ 162
   5.5. News/Blog Reporter ········ 164
   5.6. Debate Competitions ········ 165
   5.7. Volunteer Works ········ 166
   5.8. Internships ········ 168
   5.9. Other Websites ········ 169

Chapter 6 Journey of Model UN ········ 171
   6.1. John Sang-Yup Lee's Experience ········ 171
   6.2. Jong Lim's Experience ········ 184
   6.3. Rinchong Kim's Experience ········ 193
   6.4. Danny Hong's Experience ········ 195
   6.5. MaryAnn Shim's Experience ········ 201
   6.6. Gayoon Lee's Experience ········ 203
   6.7. Min Seok Park's Experience ········ 207

Chapter 7 Additional Resources ·· 209
    7.1. List of Model UN Events in Korea ····························· 209
    7.2. Glossary of Model UN Terminologies ························ 211
    7.3. Other Model UN Books & Resources ························ 215
    7.4. THIMUN Rules of Procedures ································· 219
    7.5. UNA-USA Rules of Procedures ······························· 228
    7.6. Model UN research paper ·· 263
    7.7. Author's Model UN Resume ···································· 276

Epilogue ··· 278

1, **2**, **3** … numbering represents the order of steps on how the conference proceeds.

☆, ☆☆, and ☆☆☆ roughly represent the difficulty levels of different conferences.

Preface

Model United Nations also known as MUN, is one of the most popular extra-curricular activities nowadays. Though not every student knows about Model UN in Korea, there certainly is a group of people who actively participate in the relays of varying conferences. Currently about 30 national and regional Model UN conferences are held in Korea through student run organizations, companies, and groups of schools. Countless mini- conferences are also hosted by individual clubs associated with international and public schools as well as institutions such as foreign language high schools.

I have actively participated in Korea's Model UN society for the past four years and though there may be some 'MUNers' who may know a lot more about MUN than myself, I started writing this book as not many people are getting access to MUN due to its somewhat secluded nature. The need for an update from past MUN publications was also necessary since the Model UN society in Korea had changed rapidly for the past several years. This book will cover the varying aspects that form Korea's Model UN society, ranging from participating in conferences to organizing them. Note that although there is a pool of 'MUNers' for college students, I have mainly focused on Korea's high school conferences (middle school included) as it covers a wide range of the Korea Model UN society with which I have had the most experience.

Compared to the market many years ago, the Model UN market as of 2015 is over-populated in a sense that there are too many conferences without enough participants for each. Although there have been efforts to tackle this issue, not many have proven to be successful. In this context, this book also talks about Korea's current Model UN market trend and its possible future along with some viable solutions.

The information presented in this book is largely based on my personal experience in the field and thus the contents of this book will most likely be subjective. However, I've tried to accumulate differing perspectives from highly experienced 'MUNers' to portray the information I have accumulated as accurately as possible. The information I couldn't attain first-hand was mostly excluded to mainly deal with information I attained between 2012 and 2015 while actively working in the field.

Accumulating diverse knowledge attained in the field, I worked to draft a comprehensive book that could guide starting 'MUNers' to the exciting world of Model UN. Starting delegates will be able to learn different conference proceedings and the workings of a conference. In-depth preparation skills needed for delegates, student officers, and secretariats are also included to help guide rookies step by step. Extracurricular activities in Korea that have similar grounds like Model UN have also been described in this book. I sincerely hope for the readers to get to know Model UN not only as an academic experience that will end during high school, but also as a productive experience that allows them to develop vital skills for their future.

Chapter 1
What is Model United Nations?

Model UN is a simulation of the actual United Nations and is one of the largest student activities worldwide. Participating students research the given agendas prior to a conference to write a solution paper called a resolution that benefits their assigned country's stances. There are about 30 national conferences in Korea and thousands abroad (The lists of Model UN conferences in Korea are in the appendix). Largely, there are two types of Model UN: Model UN with UNA-USA format and Model UN with the THIMUN format. In Chapter 1, I will explain how each style works along with the pros and cons of their usages. Tips I've learned regarding the usage of Rules of Procedure will also be included in this chapter so you may want to take a look even if you already know all about the procedures.

1.1. THIMUN Rules of Procedures in Korea

THIMUN Rules of Procedures is known to have originated from the actual THIMUN conference hosted by the THIMUN Foundation. It is used in THIMUN The Hague, Singapore, Qatar, Latin America, and O-MUN. My second conference in Korea was a conference called KIMC in 2012 which used the THIMUN Rules of Procedures. Frankly speaking, THIMUN Rules of Procedures are easier to follow because they have fewer rules than the UNA-USA styled format. However, the style has its cons in that it doesn't allow for a free flow of debate like that of the UNA-USA format. Though THIMUN rules may be easier to follow at first, if you experience the rules of UNA-USA, you will feel the 'rigid structure' of the THIMUN format.

Thus in Korea, not many conferences go by the THIMUN Rules of Procedures. The only ones that do so are the KIMC, HAIS MUN, KHSMUN, and a few others. But the THIMUN Rules of Procedures used in Korea are slightly different from what is used by the THIMUN Foundation. Therefore, when discussing the rules of THIMUN, I will talk about them based on the THIMUN rules in Korea. And because KIMC began in 2011 while HAIS MUN was launched in 2014, I will try to focus on KIMC rules which have a longer history.

1 Roll Call

When you go to your committee rooms, your chair will first conduct a roll call. When the chair calls your country, you have to raise your placard and say either 'present' or 'present and voting'. 'Present and voting' is different from simply saying 'present' because if you say 'present and voting', you won't be able to abstain during substantive voting procedures (substantive voting is a vote on substantive matters including votes on resolution and amendments). By saying 'present and voting', you are obliging yourself to take a firm stance by excluding your option to abstain. But because the roll call is conducted every day, you can say 'present and voting' on the first day but raise 'present' on the third day when you will need to vote on the draft-resolutions. Raising 'present and voting' on the first day may be beneficial because you will first be able to show others that you know the Rules of Procedures and secondly be able to tell others that you have a firm stance on the agenda. Of course, if your country's stance is ambivalent about the topic, you may

Delegates taking a roll call

want to abstain from saying 'present and voting'.

2 Setting the Agenda

After conducting the roll call, your committee will need to set the agenda. If there is only one topic, the chair might skip the process of setting the agenda and directly move into discussion. However, if not, one of the delegates (participants) will need to hold his/her placard high and set the motion by saying "Motion! Motion to set the agenda on agenda x". Because the first agenda that is set is usually discussed the most, you may want to raise the motion to set the agenda on which you have prepared more. To note an interesting phenomenon, not a single conference I've participated in has started its conference with agenda B; every single conference started with agenda A. So if you don't have enough time to prepare for both agendas thoroughly, you could spend more time researching on agenda A. But if agenda B appeals to you more, you should research agenda B more intensively and try to persuade other delegates to discuss agenda B first and raise a motion to discuss agenda B prior to agenda A.

3 Opening Speeches

In THIMUN formatted Model UN, an opening speech is a great way to show how well you have prepared for the conference. Delegates are usually called upon by alphabetical order to the

A delegate making a speech

podium and are given 90 seconds to state their country's stances and present some of their solutions to the committee. This is the first speech everyone in the committee is mandated to make. Therefore this is the time to analyze others and be analyzed by others. It would be imperative to grab everyone's attention and frame how you would like the conference to go. It would be great if you could brand yourself through a set of solutions and frame your position to make your own caucus later during unmoderated caucuses. To first grab the attention of others, I once wore an A4 printed flag of the nation I'm representing and distributed my position papers to other delegates before the session. Also, while others made their opening speeches, I've written notes to those who had similar stances as mine to meet during unmoderated caucuses. By communicating with others when others are not, you will be able to have a better understanding of other nations and will be able to lead them.

A typical opening speech consists of a delegate's country stance, activities the country did in accordance with its stance, several points the delegate believes is necessary for discussion, and framed solutions the delegate believes should be used to tackle the issue. The following opening speech is one I used in 2013 Canada International Model UN.

 **Opening Speech**

The People's Republic of China acknowledges the fact that Mali is having a crisis on human rights. China knows about the political instability in the south, uncertainty in the north, possibility of terrorism and continued guerilla tactics by Islamist extremists, and new conflicts between the Touaregs and the Malian government. That has been the reason why China was in favor of UNSC Resolution 2085 on 20 December 2012.

To solve the crisis in Mali, China believed that assisting regional organizations near Mali would protect Mali's sovereignty and solve the problem itself; at least to some extent. China approved UNSC Resolution 2085 because it encouraged political dialogues between Bamako, Ansar Dine, and etc. He thought that by making an effort to restrain the use of outer coercive measures, the international society would be able to provide Mali with at least some protection of its sovereignty.

But as the situation developed, French forces came to intervene in Mali. China is concerned with this fact for it might turn Mali into France's "Afghanistan", dragging nations into a prolonged conflict. China is alarmed because it legitimizes "fighting terrorism" as justification for foreign intervention in a civil war of a sovereign country. While China strongly believes that the crisis needs to be solved, he does not believe that a country should intervene in another nation without UNSC's discussion. China also hopes that France, after completing the necessaries, will pull out soon and hand over the military responsibility to the African-led mission that had been approved by the Security Council.

Through the mediation of relevant parties in regions near Mali, Mali has been making an effort to restore its constitutional rules. China hopes that the various parties will work together in completing Mali's transition process, properly resolving the crisis in the north and safeguarding national and ethnic unity. China will support the UN to protect the interests of developing countries and make greater contribution in building a world of enduring peace.

4 Forming Resolutions

In a THIMUN styled Model UN that lasts for 2~3 days, after everyone makes their speeches, the chair will give the delegates about 6 hours to write draft resolutions. Unlike UNA-USA formatted Model UNs, THIMUN style allots delegates the time to write draft resolutions. Ideally, you would have contacted people you want to work with by passing notes during the opening speeches. If not, you should hurry to find people to work with since everyone will group up in the first 10~15 minutes.

The formats of resolution differ with every conference, but the big frame works are similar. You first have the perambulatory clauses that are stated before the operative clauses. Perambulatory clauses are clauses that define the ambience of your resolution. It usually talks about the problems of the past and things delegates should consider in writing their operative clauses. The perambulatory clauses aren't discussed much in Model UN so you wouldn't need to stress about writing them. They usually aren't read during authorship speeches of a draft-resolution and aren't subject to amendments. Just keep in mind that if the

Delegates discussing resolutions in an unmoderated caucus

resolution is a solution sheet to an agenda, perambulatory clauses are what remind others of the problems.

Operative clauses are the solution part of the resolution and are thus imperative that you know how to write them. Delegates usually come out with 6~8 operative clauses per resolution and ideally there will be more operative clauses than perambulatory clauses since there should be more solutions than the number of problems. When writing operative clauses, you should think about the logic: Who is taking action? When? Where? How? Which? Why? But you shouldn't simply list all the logics in one clause; only write the essentials. Too many sub clauses, as shown in operative clause 2 of the sample resolution below, may be deleted by the chairs' discretion. Resolution writing may indeed seem highly complicated at first. However, just remind yourself that the operative clauses are a set of solutions with simplified rationales and you will be fine. Operative clauses are the solutions which your committee presents for the agenda and its sub clauses are there to help others better understand how your operative clauses work. Resolution writing will become comfortable after writing one or two resolutions.

Resolution

Sponsors: People's Republic of China
Signatories:
Topic: Re-evaluation of R2P

The United Nations Security Council,

Deeply concerned with past incidences of genocides in Rwanda and Kosovo,

Welcoming 2005 World Summit document and resolution 1674 which had been passed unanimously,

Reminding member states that R2P's original intention is for the prevention of mass violations of human rights regarding genocide, war crimes, crimes against humanity, and ethnic cleansing,

Fully Alarmed with the possibility of R2P's abuse,

Bearing in mind of UNSC resolution S/RES/1973 which deplored the failure of the Libyan incidence and other failures of the past uses of R2P,

Strongly reminding nations on UN Charter Article 2 Section 7 that national sovereignty of nations should always be respected,

Acknowledging sovereignty not only as a right but also as a responsibility that protects citizen's human rights,

Reaffirming the idea that prevention, peaceful measures and non-interceptive actions must be taken before any last extreme resort of confrontational action such as military intervention be taken,

Notes A/66/874 paragraph 20 on five lessons the UN learned from experience, being: every situation is distinct, such distinctions may lead to charges of double standards, the need for a more integrated/nuanced understanding of how the three pillars relate to, the critical role of partners, and that effective and integrated strategy is likely to involve elements of prevention,

Aware of the fact that authorization of coercive methods may cause more harm than it was intended to prevent,

Understanding that vague guidelines cannot be the sole basis for military intervention,

Expresses its appreciation with A/66/874 Chapter 3 that states that experience has shown that mediation and preventive diplomacy are most effective when different organizations work together,

Fully understanding that R2P deals with not just action against mass atrocities but also on the restoration of such crisis,

Strongly welcoming ideals and values of 'Responsibility while Protecting' and 'Responsible Protection',

Recognizing the need for timely and decisive action,

1. <u>Urges</u> the international society to devise preventive measures from mass atrocities while abiding the first pillar of R2P by means such as but not limited to:
    a) continuing and refining the early warning system of the UNGA initiated since 2010 by considering the system of the Office of the High Commissioner for Human Rights (OHCHR) and through cooperation with organizations such as having the International Court of Justice (ICJ) and International Criminal Court (ICC) investigate issues which breached human rights,

b) enhancing preventive diplomacy and good offices of the UN to settle disputes through dialogues by not having precondition attached and no political parties being excluded,
c) curbing illicit trade in small arms and light weapons by means such as but not limited to,
   i. specifying that all arms, spare parts and accessories and packing containers all bear unique stamps with codes of the country, weapons category, factory, year of manufacture, serial number, and etc. to easily track down loose weapons,
   ii. refusing to sell weapons to countries which hadn't been willing to abide by the UN Charter,
   iii. enhancing export licenses and making an end-user certificate system for better control of weapons,
   iv. encouraging the international society to propose enhanced cooperation among law enforcement agencies such as INTERPOL;
2. Calls upon peaceful means in accordance with the UN Charter when solving mass atrocities by means such as but not limited to:
   a) strengthening the role and capacity of regional organizations in areas to give out humanitarian aid by means such as but not limited to:
      i. personnel training, institution building, information and experience sharing, resource management, logistical assistance, material supplies and funding, and support for regional peace operations,

ii. strengthening coordinative mechanisms with the African Union and thus supporting the implementation of the Declaration on Enhancing UN-AU cooperation,
iii. establishing a local network of working groups dedicated to information and technical assistance for aims such as illicit arms control on a regional basis,
iv. providing opportunities for NGOs and field analysts with expertise to brief the Council,
v. abiding by peaceful measures under 2005 World Summit Document Chapter VI,

b) leaving enough space and time for a nation's autonomous reforms when the intervening states and nations subjected to R2P both believe that the best way to solve a nation's problem is to provide times for reform,

c) encouraging further development of communication between the Department of Political Affairs and peacekeeping operations along with the Department of Field Support to cooperate to have efficient discussion on R2P,

d) using effective tools in areas such as military, economic, political, and diplomatic spaces on the nations to help protect their civilians,
   i. enforcing arms embargoes and ending military cooperation along with ending training programs if the decision makers of the conflict fail to abide by the UN's decision,

    ii. having aviation bans to bring about compliance of the opposition leader and to put restrictions on travel,
    iii. enforcing legal means on deploying monitors or mediation officers or taking away diplomatic representation,
    iv. enforcing economic sanctions controlled by the advisory council composed of an amalgamation of political parties in terms of funding, aid assistance or debt relief,
    v. enacting trade restrictions on countries,
e) enhancing the ability of UN peacekeepers to carry out civilian protection mechanisms under the guidance of field commanders to increase PKO's autonomy which should be further discussed and to do the followings things such as:
    i. training peacekeepers on associated civilian protection tasks and priorities,
    ii. reducing troop rotations to ensure that peacekeeping officers would understand their mission more clearly,
    iii. permanently assigning Political Affairs or regional organization's personnel to file sites to provide them with culturally sensitive information,
    iv. accompanying multinational armies if they intervene,
    v. further discussing the issue of coercive protection of the peacekeeping forces but recognizing their need

to use active measures in protecting civilians during combat;

3. <u>Emphasize</u> the need to set certain standards in R2P to prohibit its misuse through such measures as:
   a) R2P needing both a legal authority and legitimate situation for its implementation,
   b) All rules and limits set in the resolution regarding R2P which authorizes military action to be enforced in cases which doesn't hinder the work of other UN bodies,
   c) Passing R2P related resolutions that have to do with coercive methods to be in a condition such as, but not limited to having:
      i. a clear and unambiguous mandate,
      ii. a purpose of it not being to defeat or change a regime,
      iii. maximizing protection of the civilian population,
      iv. a UN member state's priority mentioned in the resolution focused not on the resolve of the mission but on the protection of human rights,
   d) UN peacekeeping forces having a focus on eliminating root causes of conflicts to build a stable economic state with human rights;

4. <u>Reaffirms</u> the need to have restoration methods set under the second pillar of R2P in accordance with the UN Charter in means such as but not limited to:
   a) Reducing the time consuming process for NGO organizations to help restore R2P implemented areas by providing humanitarian and developmental aids,

b) Authorizing regional organizations and nations to help restore conflicts affected by R2P by such means:
   i. continuing to maintain peace and stability in the region by means other than UN security forces,
   ii. providing electoral aid and assistance including infrastructural aid, education of elections and political reforms and etc.
   iii. training regional troops to deal with terror, terrorists, and radical groups,
c) Nations that had intervened in the subjected nation be responsible for the aftermaths and to write reports on the restoration process;

5. Expresses its hope that UN member states would devise efficient and effective means in reevaluating R2P using regional organizations while bearing the UN Charter in mind to abide by the three pillars from prevention to restoration;
6. Resolves to remain actively seized on the matter.

5 Flow of Debate

Initially the chair will call upon delegates who have raised their placards to speak on the podium to discuss the given agenda. But after someone raises a motion to introduce a draft resolution and if that motion passes, the 'main submitter' of that draft resolution will make a 4 minute speech called the authorship speech on why his/her resolution should pass (a main submitter is someone who contributed the most to the writing of that resolution and presents it). Note that in some conferences, only one resolution may pass in each committee and usually the draft resolution that had been introduced first passes as it is discussed the most. Therefore it would be wise to introduce one's resolution before those of others.

6 Amendment

After a draft resolution has been introduced to the floor and after the main submitter has made his/her 4 minute authorship speech, delegates should only discuss matters regarding the draft resolution. If someone wants to change some contents of the draft resolution, one may request an amendment sheet to either strike/change/add onto the draft resolution. When writing an amendment, you shouldn't be talking about minimal errors such as grammar mistakes but should deal with its fundamental ideas. For instance, if you believe that GNP, instead of GDP, should be the standard in deciding whether to give aid or not, you might want to make an amendment. But if it's about some awkward wordings, you may want to make a different amendment that could impact the draft resolution more significantly. In some conferences there is a thing called a 'friendly amendment' where the writers of the draft resolution can change the content they want to change anytime. This method has its benefits since the time consuming process of making amendments will disappear.

Delegates in session

However, as a 'friendly amendment' can also be used for the benefit of just a small amount of people in the committee, most Korean Model UN conferences don't have 'friendly amendments' in their Rules of Procedures.

7 Passing Resolutions

After finishing debates and making amendments, a delegate may raise the motion to move into the previous question. Unlike UNA-USA formatted Model UN conferences which need to first close the debate and then vote on the resolution (motion to close debate and motion to vote on the resolution), THIMUN formatted Model UN conferences have the two motions combined and by passing this motion, the debate will be closed and the committee will directly move into the voting procedure of the resolution.

1.2. UNA-USA Rules of Procedures in Korea

UNA-USA rules are the most prevalent rules in Korea's Model UN conferences. It also turned out that students like the UNA-USA rules better when I conducted a survey of high school students who have participated in Model UN in Korea. But because THIMUN rules have their benefits too, for instance having the opening speeches so that everyone can participate, some Model UNs that go by the UNA-USA rules have now incorporated some parts of the THIMUN procedures. Thus one trend of Korea Model UN conferences include the blending of THIMUN procedures with UNA-USA rules.

※ Some reasons why students prefer UNA-USA Rules of Procedure over the THIMUN format include:
1. One can exchange more ideas with other delegates before writing resolutions
2. The conference feels more "free" and "unrestricted"
3. Delegates can speak more by having unmoderated caucuses
4. Writing position papers can clear one's thoughts
5. It is more fun using motions to lead the debate where one wants it to go instead of following the structured format of THIMUN procedures.

One of the most significant differences between the UNA-USA and THIMUN formats is that UNA-USA format requires something called a 'position paper'. This paper is a 1~3 page document that delegates send to their committee chairs through e-mail 1~2 weeks before the conference. This paper, similar to that of an opening speech in THIMUN formatted conferences, should include a nation's stance, past UN actions, the nation's past and current actions along with its future solutions. Though writing this paper may be an arduous task, you should be able to summarize your research into a 1~3 page long paper. Position papers come in handy to quickly draw facts during a conference and may be useful to use for an opening speech on the first day of the conference. Just remember to cite sources before submitting it to your chairs.

 **Position Paper**

The DPRK used to be a nation that also promoted nuclear non-proliferation during the 1980s. However, it started violating the terms made between countries more often and eventually refused to be inspected by IAEA, later causing its withdrawal from the NPT in January 2003. The DPRK states that it had done so because its security had been threatened with nuclear weapons remaining in ROK's province. While one of the conditions for the 1991 Joint Declaration of the

Denuclearization of the Korean Peninsula was a complete denuclearization of both Koreas, nuclear weapons of the US still remained in the ROK. The Agreed Framework signed on October 21, 1994 had also been ruined by this deficiency. But while the People's Republic of China does believe that the DPRK's reason for making its statement was valid, it is completely against DPRK's actions that threatens other nations. First, China believes that the DPRK shouldn't have left the NPT. As the UN Security Council declared that the proliferation of all weapons of mass destruction constitutes a threat to international peace and security, there shouldn't be a nation that withdraws from the NPT. The DPRK should have firmly requested the US to remove its nuclear weapons from ROK instead of violating the existing treaty.

With the DPRK threatening other nations to use the DPRK's nuclear missiles, the United Nations passed resolution 1718 to impose various forms of sanctions on DPRK. But as the DPRK conducted its second nuclear test on May 25th, we passed UNSC resolution 1874 in 2009, reinforcing resolution 1718. Resolution 2087 has also been passed to sanction DPRK, resolution 2094 being the most recent sanction in 2013. China agreed to these resolutions despite its concern for the DPRK's economic stability because it believes that the DPRK should abide by the NPT terms. China will not abandon the DPRK. This nation clearly has shown this through its various actions such as having the bilateral summit in 2011. However, China believes that the DPRK should follow resolutions passed in the UN Security Council. And to do so, China believes that multilateral talks should be promoted between nations. This nation calls for an emergency session of six party talks to exchange views on major issues of concern. While the US, Japan, and ROK rejected China's call in 2010, China believes that the frozen talks should be revived. As nations like Libya and Iran have shown their change of national stance, China hopes for a change in the DPRK's stance.

To comprehensively deal with the situation of the DPRK, factors such as chemical and biological weapons should also be addressed during the conference. According to the International Crisis Group's (ICG) 2009 report, the Korean People's Army possesses chemical weapon (CW) arsenals up to 5,000 tons. ICG stated that while the stockpiles do not appear to be increasing, it is already sufficient to inflict massive civilian casualties. We shouldn't just be cautious about WMDs. The DPRK currently hasn't signed the Chemical Weapons Convention (CWC), Biological and Toxin Weapons Convention (BTWC), or the Geneva Protocol which prohibits the use of chemical and biological weapons in war. As the ROK had dismantled its entire chemical weapons program in 2008, DPRK should also do so for the sake of the stability of the Korean peninsula.

In creating solutions for the situation in the DPRK, nations shouldn't just argue about their previous actions. As previous solutions failed, a more efficient solution is needed. Thus China proposes five solutions. First, China believes that NPT itself should be discussed as to its enforcement. To make a peaceful world, non-nuclear proliferation is needed and thus should be enforced upon all member states of the United Nations. A review conference for the NPT is currently planned to be held in 2015; China believes that its enforcement may be discussed shortly in GC 2014 to deal with the DPRK's situation. Secondly, denuclearization of the Korean peninsula should come to action. There have been many troubles in the course of enforcing complete denuclearization since 1991. However, since it seems that the DPRK is starting to get more out of control with the seemingly unstable Kim Jung Un regime, China sees the urgent need for Korea's complete denuclearization. Thirdly, we should devise measures in stabilizing DPRK. While we had made some extreme measures in sanctioning DPRK, their purpose was only to stop the DPRK from continuing its ongoing nuclear experiments. Looking at the vast majority of the citizens under the poverty line, China had been active and is willing to continue to be active in reviving its economy. Fourthly, nations should not overlook the possible danger in CWs and BTWs and thus should talk about implementing CWCs and BTWC in Korea. UN Special Commission (UNSCOM) should conduct a full investigation to first determine the regarding status quo. Lastly, talks should come back to the table. All talks had been frozen as the US took the position of not talking with the DPRK without its concrete action for change. While the basis of calling for the DPRK's change was intriguing, things have only become worse after several years of its enforcement. Nations should not be stubborn with their ideas. If the US asks for any preconditions, the DPRK will also do so as well. Solutions won't be achieved by making preconditions. China hopes to talk with every nation to discuss further solutions in dealing with the current crisis. As a member state of the UN that believes in its ideals, China longs for an effective resolution that will promote peace in the Korean peninsula.

Another aspect in which the UNA-USA format and THIMUN format differs is with its forms of debate. While a THIMUN formatted conference has the minimum diversity regarding points and motions, UNA-USA formatted conferences have 10~30 different points and motions. Although this factor makes it hard for rookie delegates to follow UNA-USA conferences, the flow of debate becomes more dynamic. I have provided you with the points and motions chart for a typical Model UN conference in Korea below. But because it will be very hard to understand the usage of each point and motion through simple reading, I recommend participating in an actual Model UN conference.

Note that the Rules of Procedures mentioned in this book are not intended to help you understand how to do Model UN instantly. This section is here to help you look for critical parts of the rules during the conference. I intended to make it so that by reading this book before the conference, you will be able to have an overall picture regarding where the conference is moving and how to use the rules for your benefit.

The following chart describes the varying points and motions in a UNA-USA formatted conference.

Point of Personal Privilege	▸ Raised to express discomfort during the conference (ex. Temperature, audibility) ▸ May interrupt another speaker's speech when it has to do with his/her audibility
Point of Order	▸ Raised to correct a chair when a chair deviates from the Rules of Procedure (It would be better to raise it as a point of inquiry since this motion may be considered rude)
Point of Parliamentary Inquiry	▸ Raised to ask questions about conference proceedings to the chair
Point of Notice	▸ A note given by the chair to a delegate to inform something
Point of Clarification	▸ Raised after a delegate finishes speaking to ask about terminology used during his/her speech

Point of Information	▸ Raised by a speaker to use the remaining speaking time for Question and Answers
Motion to set the Agenda	▸ Raised to set the agenda when there is none on the floor ▸ Is followed by 2 speakers for and against
Motion to set the Speaking Time	▸ Raised to change the current speaking time
Motion for a Roll Call	▸ Raised to count a quorum
Motion to move into an Unmoderated Caucus	▸ Raised to discuss freely with each other (ex. Writing resolutions and caucusing) ▸ Its purpose and total duration time should be stated
Motion to move into a Moderated Caucus	▸ Raised to focus on a specific topic or to accelerate the debate ▸ Its purpose, total duration time, and individual speaking time should be stated
Motion to Introduce Draft Resolution	▸ Raised to officially introduce a draft resolution that had been approved by the chair
Motion to Introduce an Amendment	▸ Raised to officially introduce an amendment that had be approved by the chair
Motion to Table Debate	▸ Raised to temporarily stop discussion on the current agenda/resolution/amendment to discuss other matters ▸ Is followed by 2 speakers for and against
Motion to Resume Debate	▸ Raised to resume a debate that had been tabled, or postponed ▸ Is followed by 2 speakers for and against
Motion to Close Debate	▸ Raised to close the discussion on an amendment/resolution ▸ Is followed by 2 speakers against ▸ If it passes, a motion to vote on an amendment/resolution will be raised by someone to vote on amendment/resolution

Motion to Adjourn the Session	▸ Raised to temporarily end the session for reasons such as a lunch or break
Motion to Adjourn the Meeting	▸ Raised at the end of all sessions to finish the official discussion on the agenda
Motion to Suspend the Rules	▸ Raised to suspend a rule mentioned in the Rules of Procedure ▸ Requires the approval of a secretariat

A delegate raising his placard

1 Roll Call & 2 Setting the Agenda

As Roll Calls and Setting the Agenda which were mentioned in the THIMUN format aren't different from those of UNA-USA format, I will focus on the difference regarding the Flow of Debate.

(Remember that specific Rules of Procedures vary by

conferences and the rules mentioned here only include the general rules used by most conferences).

3 Flow of Debate

There are mainly three types of debate in UNA-USA formatted Model UN conferences: moderated debate (moderated caucus), unmoderated caucus, and general debate. The default mode of debate is the general debate. This debate is the debate THIMUN uses and you can raise your placard to be listed on the 'general speakers list.' When it is your turn to speak according to the list, you will have 90 seconds to speak at the podium and will be able to yield the remaining time for points of information or to another delegate or back to the chair. If you yield the remaining speaking time for point of informations, other delegates will get a chance to ask you questions about your speech and you will have a chance to answer them. Stating that you are open to any and all points of information for your remaining speaking time may imply that you aren't afraid of questions because you know what you are talking and may help you during award considerations. Even if you are stuck on a question after accepting it, you can simply tell the inquirer that you will answer that question in a note form and move on answering other questions. If you yield the remaining time to another delegate, the next delegate can come up to the podium and speak for the remaining time. Lastly if you yield your time back to the chair, it will be the same as exhausting your speaking time and you can simply go back to your seat.

However because moving up to the podium is time consuming and because people listed on the back of the speakers' list can't speak, another form of debate may be useful in certain circumstances: moderated debate (moderated caucus). Moderated debate is a form of debate in which someone can simply stand after being recognized by the chair to speak for the time and purpose set by the delegate who raised this motion. To have this form of debate, you need to state the motion's total duration time, individual speaking time, and the purpose of the motion. For instance, you may say "Motion! Motion to have a moderated debate for the duration of 15 minutes, individual speaking time 60 seconds for the purpose of discussing x". Note that you need to state the motion's purpose when moving for a moderated caucus. Thus if you are in a moderated debate and someone speaks about something that is irrelevant to the reason why the motion for the moderated debate was raised, you can inquire your chair on whether the speech made by the other delegate was appropriate or was 'in order'. Moderated debate is very useful to frame the debate the way you want it to be and to quicken the debate by having many people speak in a short period of time. If you feel that more opinions should be heard, you can set the individual speaking time to 30 seconds in the motion your raise.

The third and last style of discussion in a UNA-USA format is called the 'unmoderated caucus'. This motion can be raised by

Delegates having a moderated caucus

stating a motion's total duration time and its purpose. For instance, you may state "Motion! Motion to move into an unmoderated caucus for the total duration time of 20 minutes for the purpose of drafting resolution." This motion is typically used to create time to write draft resolutions (it works like the official resolution writing time in the THIMUN procedure) but can also be used to discuss other matters that go beyond draft-resolution writings without the restrictions of speaking time. You can sit, stand, or walk and roam around the conference room to interact with other delegates. There is no speaking time so you can speak all you want. You may even use this time as a time to go to the restroom.

Unmoderated caucus is mostly, however, a time of tension for award-seekers because the first unmoderated caucus will decide who writes what in the draft-resolution. When the first unmoderated caucus is motioned and passes, you would be able to see other delegates gathering around one delegate. That delegate is most likely the delegate who had spoken the most and had presented the most thought-provoking solutions to the committee. As people gather around that delegate, he/she will most likely open his/her laptop and jot down solutions other delegates are telling him/her. When that is going on, some delegates 'outside the circle' will be left out and you will also be able to see another delegate gathering them to his/her table. Though those who write resolutions don't necessarily become Best Delegate awardees, because best delegates are those who lead others and bring compromises, it is highly likely for the person in the center of the circle to win the awards. Winning awards isn't everything in Model UN; but to win an award, you will need to use an unmoderated caucus to your advantage. I would further explain about the award winning process later in this book.

4 Amendment & 5 Passing Resolutions

The amendment and the resolution process between the UNA-USA and THIMUN formats are similar with only two differences. Firstly, unlike THIMUN formatted conferences which almost always have the main submitter come up to the podium to read his/her resolution (the authorship speech), some UNA-USA conferences don't have main submitters, instead they have something called 'sponsors'. The sponsors of a resolution are those who had contributed themselves to the writings of a resolution. And though usually only one person speaks to present a caucus' authorship speech (who would be a main submitter in THIMUN), other sponsors may be on the podium along with the leader of the bloc to answer questions that may be raised by other delegates during the question session that comes after the authorship speech in UNA-USA format. I personally think that this system of having sponsors is better because then the delegates wouldn't need to fight over who becomes the main submitter and there will be rooms left for other delegates to participate in the writings of a resolution. The second major difference between THIMUN and UNA-USA formatted conferences regard voting procedure on resolutions. In a UNA-USA conference, a committee will need to first close the debate on the resolution to move to vote on a resolution.

Chapter 2
Model UN of Korea

The national flag of Korea

Attending conferences and hearing from other MUNers, I realized that there were several distinct Model UN societies in Korea that do not mix very well with each other. The reasons for this seem to vary from area and language to organizations that host Model UN conferences. I researched but never found a single paper explaining this trend. So while discussing domestic Model UN conferences in Korea, I will try to articulate why this phenomenon (if it happens at all) occurs and try my best to identify the trends of Model UN in Korea. This chapter explains how Korea's Model UN society works and discusses various parts of Korea's Model UN society.

2.1. Routes of Participation

Region and Language

2014년도 상반기 지역별 모의유엔 프로그램 안내

지역	일자	프로그램
원주	7.2 – 7.5	전국 대학생 모의유엔 회의
수원	7.18 – 7.20	KIMUN WORKSHOP
서울	7.20	HAISMUN
인천	7.24 – 7.26	IMUN
수원	7.25 – 7.27	KAYMUN
서울	7.26 – 7.28	SIGMUN
서울	7.28 – 7.30	Seoul Summit
수원	7.28 – 8.3	WFUNA 청소년 캠프
서울	7.31 – 8.2	GLIS MUN
제주	8.7 – 8.9	JOINED MUN
창원	8.8 – 8.10	CAMUN
서울	8.8 – 8.10	KHSMUN
서울	8.8 – 8.10	KIMC
서울	8.9	HIMUN
서울	8.11 – 8.13	MUNCCC
광주	10.24 – 10.25	GYMUN

Distribution of Model UN conferences in Korea

Korea's Model UN society is largely divided into two regions: Seoul and the southern areas of Korea. Incheon and Seoul are connected by subways and thus MUNers in Incheon are frequently seen at Model UN conferences held in Seoul. Even students from Jeju Island fly to come to Model UN conferences held in Seoul (usually students who attend international schools in Jeju Island). However, as it takes 3~4 hour trips by train to come to Seoul conferences from southern areas, not many southerners are seen at Seoul conferences.

As the official language of most conferences that are held in Seoul is English, the language barrier also seems to keep out students in south who haven't had enough English education from attending Seoul conferences. (There is a big gap of English education in Korea). And thus the Model UN society in Seoul and the southern parts of Korea have evolved differently. While Model UN in Seoul uses English as the working language for most of its committees, southern conferences almost always use Korean as its official language. It is interesting to note that conferences like CAMUN and MUNNEO use English in their conference names though they do not have English committees; it may be due to the fact that Model UN had spread from Seoul which only uses English in its conference titles.

Anyhow, another factor that is different between Seoul and other conferences is that while Seoul conferences select staff members 1~2 months before the conference, some other conferences choose their staffs while picking their secretariats. Seoul conferences seem to have a structuralized, hierarchical positioning while other conferences have a bit more interaction between secretariat positions at different levels. It is also interesting to see that while the committees in Seoul conferences consist of the usual committees like UNHCR, UNDP, UNGA and etc., conferences outside of Seoul also hosts committees like IOCs or even FIFA. This phenomenon can be explained when looking at the fact that Seoul conferences have more history then other conferences. It seems that by having a set of standard for long time, the structure of the Model UN in Seoul has become more consolidated than that of other regions.

Different Model UN Organizations

There are numerous Model UN organizations in Korea. Some are 100% student led, some are led by a newspaper company, and some are a mix of other entities. Most colleges have their own Model UN club which hosts Model UN conferences for college or high school students. KIOSS at Korea University for instance hosts the Korea Model UN and YDMUN at Yonsei University hosts Yonsei Model UN. Here, I will focus on Model UN organizations that somehow affect the high school Model UN society in Korea- specifically focusing on organizations that go beyond simply making a conference as that will be no different from typical secretariat organizations of Model UN conferences. Note that as some organizations are dormant or aren't advertised much, there may be other organizations that I have missed to acknowledge. The following organizations are those which a fair amount of MUNers know.

University-led Organization

KIC Model UN Secretariats
(http://www.kicmun.org/)

I have mentioned KIC Model UN Secretariats while excluding other university organizations because KICMUN, unlike other university organizations, organizes the Model UN workshop with the World Federation of United Nations Association (WFUNA) and hosts WFUNA Youth Camp in Korea for high school students. It also is in partnership with UNA-USA and sends the Best Delegate awardees to Global Classroom International Model UN held in New York every year as part of Korea's National Model UN Team. Not only that, KICMUN has initiated an outreach program since 2014 to help high school students learn about Model UN. KICMUN which has started in 2008, is one of the largest university led organizations that affects high school Model UN society.

Student Led Organizations

Model UN Association of Korea
(http://www.munak.org/main/index.php)

Model UN Association of Korea was founded in 2014, but actually originates from an internet café (http://cafe.naver.com/theworldwithus) that has operated since 2011. It used to be a Model

UN café for a high school club. But as the café manager Hosung Ahn started to post valuable Model UN contents for everyone, students from other schools started to register to become members and the café started to become the largest Model UN internet platform in Korea. I personally registered to become a member in 2012 and worked as its Vice President since 2013. As of July in 2015, there are currently 1,423 members registered and the café has turned into a platform that provides Model UN information. A website was constructed for MUNAK and 16 secretariats update the necessary information. I check the Question and Answer bulletin in the internet café at least once a day so if you have any questions, you can write them on the board and I'll answer them. I've written some Model UN tips a few years ago; if you want to check that out, you can see them in the Tips bulletin of the café. The following are results of MUNAK activities in 2014.

2014 1st semester Model UN conferences in Korea

중고등학생 모의유엔대회

월	날짜	대회명
5월	5.16 – 5.18	YMUN: Korea 2014
6월	5.31 – 6.1	HADMUN 2014
7월	6.30 – 7.4	WIMUN 2014
	7.10 – 7.11	Model UN HRC 2014
	7.20	HAISMUN
	7.24 – 7.26	IMUN
	7.26 – 7.28	SIGMUN
	7.31 – 8.2	GLIS MUN 9
8월	8.8 – 8.10	제3회 CAMUN
	8.8 – 8.10	KHSMUN VIII
	8.8 – 8.10	2014 KIMC
	8.11 – 8.13	MUNCCC

대학생 모의유엔대회

월	날짜	대회명
7월	7.2 – 7.5	제20회 전국대학생모의유엔회의
	7.28 – 7.30	Seoul Summit 2014

모의유엔 교육 프로그램

월	날짜	프로그램명
7월	7.18 – 7.20	KIMUN WORKSHOP IV
8월	7.28 – 8.3	제3회 WFUNA 청소년 캠프

한국모의유엔협회
Model United Nations Association of Korea

** 추후 각 대회 사정에 따라 일정이 변경 될 수 있습니다 **

2014 2nd semester Model UN conferences in Korea

분류별 모의유엔 모집

구분	날짜	모집명
사무국	08.06 – 08.17	GLIS MUN X 사무국 모집
사무국	– 08.17	제 3회 IMUN 사무국 모집
의장단		GC: Seoul 2015 의장단 모집
스태프	07.14 – 08.20	GC: Seoul 2015 데일리 모집
스태프		GC: Seoul 2015 봉사자 모집
사무국	– 08.22	제 4회 CAMUN 사무국 모집
의장단		제 4회 CAMUN 의장단 모집
사무국	– 08.30	HADMUN 6기 사무국 모집
의장단	08.18 – 08.31	제 2회 AKYD 의장단 모집

2014 Model UN conferences by agenda

PEACE & SECURITY
Conflicts, Disputes and Political Stabilization | Special Politics and Security | Sovereignty | Military Weapons of Mass Destruction

ECONOMY & DEVELOPMENT
Millennium Development Goals (MDGs) and Sustainable Development | Transportation and Technology Energy and Natural Resources | Finance | Growth, Empowerment and Redistribution

ENVIRONMENT & HEALTH
Global Warming and Climate Change | Environmental Hazards | Biodiversity | Deforestation | Health

HUMAN RIGHTS
Protection of Human Rights | Children | Women | Refugees | Human Trafficking | Humanitarian Assistance

EDUCATION & SOCIETY
Education | Cultural Heritage | Sports | People with Disabilities

UNITED NATIONS
Security Council Reform

PEACE & SECURITY - #1

		Conflicts, Disputes and Political Stabilization
GLIS MUN	7.31 – 8.2	Ways to Instill a Stable Central Government in Somalia
		Settlement of the Dispute regarding the Ownership of the Pacific Islands
		소말리아 무정부상태 해결과 국민 안정화를 위한 국제사회의 논의
		동아시아 해양영토분쟁 해결 방안 모색을 위한 국제적 논의
		중동 민주화 운동의 평화적 해결과 대응을 위한 국제적 차원의 논의
HAIS MUN	7.20	Establishment of Concrete Support Measures for the Aftermath of the Crisis in Syria
KAYMUN	7.25 – 7.27	국가분쟁 예방을 위한 국제적 협력
KHSMUN	8.8 – 8.10	UN's Involvement in Israeli-Palestinian Conflict and Disarmament between the Two Countries
		Invasion of Crimea by the Russian Army
		The Situation in DPRK

Chapter 2. Model UN of Korea | 43

Seoul Summit	7.28 - 7.30	Situation in Crimean Peninsula
		Measures to alleviate territorial disputes in South China Sea

Special Politics and Security		
CAMUN	8.8 - 8.10	전 세계적인 테러확산 방지 방안에 대한 범국가적 논의
GLIS MUN	7.31 - 8.2	Establishing Consensus on the Extent of Collectable Information for Security
IMUN	7.24 - 7.26	Designing a Global Code of Conduct on Cyber Warfare
		Preventing Militarization of the Arctic
NMUN Korea	7.2 - 7.5	UN Strategy to Prevent Mass Atrocities
SIGMUN	7.26 - 7.28	Setting Measures to Prevent Criminal Activity Occurring in the Deep Web

PEACE & SECURITY - #2

Sovereignty		
SIGMUN	7.26 - 7.28	Reaching a Consensus on International Intervention in Domestic Matters

Military		
GLIS MUN	7.31 - 8.2	Discussing the Global Deliberation of Military Spending
SIGMUN	7.26 - 7.28	Establishing Agreement on the Use of Unmanned Aerial Vehicles

Weapons of Mass Destruction		
GLIS MUN	7.31 - 8.2	핵 확산방지와 핵 군축을 위한 국제적 논의와 제재
HADMUN	5.31 - 6.1	안전보장이사회 결의 1540호의 문제점에 대한 보완 및 실질적 이행방안 모색
KHSMUN	8.8 - 8.10	The Reduction of Nuclear Warheads around the World
NMUN Korea	7.2 - 7.5	Ways to Strengthen the UN Sanction System to Address the Proliferation of WMD
Seoul Summit	7.28 - 7.30	Coordinating Efforts to Denuclearize and Prevent Proliferation of Nuclear Weapons in the Asia-Pacific

ECONOMY & DEVELOPMENT

Millennium Development Goals (MDGs) and Sustainable Development		
GLIS MUN	7.31 - 8.2	Setting a Guideline for the Post-2015 Development Agenda
IMUN	7.24 - 7.26	Measures to Accelerate Sustainable Development in Developing Countries
		Ways to collect and allocate the fund for sustainable development of nuclear energy
NMUN Korea	7.2 - 7.5	지속가능개발목표를 위한 유엔 공개작업반의 19개 중점분야 중 Post-2015 개발목표로 반영될 10개 목표 선정

Transportation and Technology		
GLIS MUN	7.31 – 8.2	Discussing Milestones for the Development of Futuristic Transportation Systems to Further Increase Economic Efficiency
HADMUN	5.31 – 6.1	차세대 항공교통관리시스템의 구축을 위한 국제적 합의 도출 및 구체적 이행 방안 마련
HAIS MUN	7.20	Establishing a Consensus on the Appropriate Implementation of Intellectual Property Systems

Energy and Natural Resources		
IMUN	7.24 – 7.26	Provision of Modern Fuel and Electricity in Developing Countries
		Promoting Feasible Management of Nuclear Energy or Spent Nuclear Fuel
		Finding Avenues to Mediate Uneven Distribution of Natural Resources

Finance		
GLIS MUN	7.31 – 8.2	Installing International Regulations Related to Distribution and Accommodation of Cyber Currencies
HADMUN	5.31 – 6.1	국제 금융 시스템 안정 및 시장 질서 유지를 위한 헤지펀드의 범세계적 규제 가이드라인 마련
Seoul Summit	7.28 – 7.30	Countering Money Laundering and Promoting Judicial Cooperation to Enhance International Cooperation
SIGMUN	7.26 – 7.28	Reaching a Consensus on the Appropriate Implementation of Structural Adjustment Programs

Growth, Empowerment and Redistribution		
GLIS MUN	7.31 – 8.2	Coming Up with Measures to Reduce Income Brackets for More Equal Distribution of Worldwide Income along with Establishing National Capacity Initiatives
		개발도상국 고용증대를 위한 국제적 차원의 논의
		남반구와 북반구 간의 경제력 차이 해결방안 모색을 위한 국제사회의 논의
IMUN	7.24 – 7.26	Reforming the Highly Indebted Countries Initiative
Seoul Summit	7.28 – 7.30	Promoting Economic and Social Development in Post-Conflict Regions

ENVIRONMENT & HEALTH

Global Warming and Climate Change		
CAMUN	8.8 – 8.10	Re-Evaluating Previous Methods of Solving Issues Regarding Climate Change
GLIS MUN	7.31 – 8.2	Creating a Comprehensive Plan to Combat the Excessive Rise of Sea Levels
		지구 온난화 발생과 이에 따른 환경 파괴의 해결책 논의
HAIS MUN	7.20	Discussing Measures to Solve Global Warming and Depletion of the Ozone Layer
		Implementation of Integrated Policies for the Lower Economically Developed Country (LEDC) facing Threat from Global Warming
KHSMUN	8.8 – 8.10	Solving the Arctic Crisis

MUNCCC	8.11 – 8.13	Greenhouse Gas Reduction
		Climate Change and Adaptation
		Global Green Growth Institute (GGGI)
		Global Climate Fund

Environmental Hazards

| GLIS MUN | 7.31 – 8.2 | Ways to Effectively Manage and Dispose Radioactive Waste |
| SIGMUN | 7.26 – 7.28 | Discussing Ways to Eliminate the Production and Use of Persistent Organic Pollutants |

Biodiversity

| SIGMUN | 7.26 – 7.28 | Devising Measures to Promote Biodiversity |

Deforestation

| IMUN | 7.24 – 7.26 | Mitigating Deforestation and Promoting Sustainable Forest Management |

Health

| SIGMUN | 7.26 – 7.28 | Establishing Measures to Insure Food Safety |
| | | Devising Methods to Improve Medical Infrastructure in LEDCs |

HUMAN RIGHTS

Protection of Human Rights

GLIS MUN	7.31 – 8.2	Discussing International Action on the Enforcement of Minimum Human Rights, specifically regarding the Situation in the Democratic People's Republic of Korea
		Placing a Guarantee of Minimum Standard for Living for LGBT Couples
IMUN	7.24 – 7.26	Effective Measures to Protect Human Rights of Foreign Workers
KHSMUN	8.8 – 8.10	Creating Global Governance to Combat All Forms of Extrajudicial Punishment
		Addressing Human Rights Depravation in Sub-Saharan Africa

Children

IMUN	7.24 – 7.26	Abolition of Child Exploitation in the Third World Countries
KHSMUN	8.8 – 8.10	Establishing and Protecting the Human Rights of Children in Post Disaster Areas
SIGMUN	7.26 – 7.28	Preparing a Roadmap to Address Children Exploitation

Women

| GLIS MUN | 7.31 – 8.2 | Addressing the Immediate Need for Governmental Compensation to Women Sexually Exploited during Armed Conflicts |

Refugees

| KAYMUN | 7.25 – 7.27 | 난민 기본권 신장 |

| SIGMUN | 7.26 – 7.28 | Pursuing the Recognition of Types and Forms to Expand Enforcement of the Rights of Refugees |

Human Trafficking

| GLIS MUN | 7.31 – 8.2 | Discussing International Regulations related to Human Trafficking to Stop the Commercial Exploitation of Human Beings |
| Seoul Summit | 7.28 – 7.30 | Resolving Prostitution and Human Trafficking in East Europe |

Humanitarian Assistance

| HADMUN | 5.31 – 6.1 | 중앙아프리카공화국을 비롯한 아프리카 내의 내전으로 발생하는 기근 및 구호식량 운송 문제의 개선방안 모색 |
| IMUN | 7.24 – 7.26 | Avenues to Effectively Deliver Relief Supplies to Countries in Need |

EDUCATION & SOCIETY

Education

CAMUN	8.8 – 8.10	지속가능 발전교육(ESD)을 통한 전 세계 지속가능발전 향상과 ESD의 발전방법 논의
GLIS MUN	7.31 – 8.2	세계사 교육에 대한 국제 기준의 확립
Seoul Summit	7.28 – 7.30	Promoting Women's Access to Education and Training, especially in the fields of Science and Technology in Developing Nations Resolving the Education Crisis in Sub-Saharan Africa using Technology

Cultural Heritage

GLIS MUN	7.31 – 8.2	분쟁 지역의 학술, 문화 유산 보호 체제
IMUN	7.24 – 7.26	Preserving Linguistic Diversity and Protecting Endangered Languages Means of Prohibiting and Preventing the Illicit Trade of Cultural Property
KHSMUN	8.8 – 8.10	Strengthening Crime Prevention and Criminal Justice Responses to Protect Cultural Property, especially with Regard to its Trafficking

Sports

| IMUN | 7.24 – 7.26 | Enhancing the Sports Diplomatic Power in Developing Nations

Finding Measures to Activate Worldwide Sporting Events for the Differently-abled |

People with Disabilities

| HAIS MUN | 7.20 | Establishing Social Infrastructures that Fit for the Needs of the Handicapped |
| IMUN | 7.24 – 7.26 | Finding Measures to Activate Worldwide Sporting Events for the Differently-abled |

UNITED NATIONS

Security Council Reform

| NMUN Korea | 7.2 – 7.5 | 포괄적인 유엔안보리 개혁을 위한 진전 방안 |
| Seoul Summit | 7.28 – 7.30 | Modifications on the Security Council Bylaws |

 **KIMC High School Union** (http://cafe.naver.com/hikimc)

KIMC High School Union or Korea International Model Congress High School Union is Korea's largest high school Model UN association. It started as a KIMC conference funded by Joongang Ilbo Newspaper Company but stopped working with it in 2014 and has become a 100% student led organization. About 30 high schools have been its members since 2011 and a total of 2,110 students are members to its internet café as of 2015. To become a member of KIMC, you need to organize a group of students in a school and apply to the KIMC High School Union. But because only one organization per school can be registered as a member of KIMC High School Union, a club can only be registered under the condition that there isn't another club at that school that has already been registered. The registration period comes bi-annually at the start of the school year and just after summer break. If you become a member school of this union, you will need to read a news article and write your opinions about that article once every week. Also, you will need to participate in an off-line meeting where you get to meet other representatives of other school's Model UN clubs. You also get a chance to organize a winter Model UN conference with the secretariats from other schools.

2014 KIMC High School Union school representatives

2015 KIMC poster

Global Talent Raising Operation
(http://cafe.naver.com/global963)

Global Talent Raising Operation was founded in 2013 and is in the process of becoming a company as of 2015. There are currently about seven people on its executive board, and its president, Jimin Kim, is working to bridge the gap between Seoul and southern Model UN conferences by exchanging secretariats. The picture below is an introduction of GTRO.

제 1회 창원 청소년 모의유엔 개최를 시작으로 활동을 시작한 글로벌인재육성사업단 GTRO 는 수도권에 집중된 모의 컨퍼런스, 정책토론대회 등의 활동을 지방학생들 에게도 제공해주기 위하여 2013년에 설립되었습니다. 청소년의 다양한 활동 보장으로 학생들의 다양한 경험에 대한 기회를 제공하여 장기적으로 글로벌 시대에 모두를 이끌어 갈 수 있는 인재를 육성하는 것을 목표로 삼고 있습니다. 글로벌인재육성사업단 GTRO는 설립부터 지금까지 많은 대회들을 주최,주관 또는 후원하며 학생들이 더욱 많은 경험을 할 수 있도록 노력하고 있습니다.

창원 청소년 모의유엔(CAMUN) 1회 주최
국제 평등 비전 모의유엔(MUNIEVU) 1회 공동주최
창원 청소년 모의유엔(CAMUN) 2회 주최
진주 청소년 모의유엔(JYMUN) 1기 주관
HAIS MUNI: The Start 후원
창원 청소년 모의유엔(CAMUN) 3회 주최
신 평등 모의유엔(MUNNEO) 1회 주최
UTOPIA AGORA of Diplomacy (UAD) 후원
Student International Government Model United Nations (SIGMUN) 1회 후원
대한민국 청소년 모의 국제재판 대회 1회 공동주최

GTRO introduction

Under the idea to provide an equal educational opportunity for students in the south, GTRO focuses its operations in the southern parts of Korea and has hosted numerous Model UN conferences including MUNNEO, CAMUN, JYMUN, and many more. GTRO also sponsors new found Model UN conferences and has sponsored HAIS MUN, SIGMUN, and a few other conferences between 2014 and 2015. It is one of the biggest Model UN organizations in the southern parts of Korea and one of the few organizations that works to bridge the gap between Seoul and southern Model UNs (GTRO internet café above hasn't been updated and a new website is currently under construction). The following posters are posters of conferences hosted by GTRO.

A conference sponsored by GTRO

A conference sponsored by GTRO

Korea Model UN Workshop Summit
(http://munws.dothome.co.kr/xe/)

Korea Model UN Workshop Summit (MUNWS) is an organization that hosts Model UN workshops in Korea. It was founded in 2014 and has recruited members from all over Korea to open Model UN workshops in different regions. It isn't as big as the KICMUN Workshop but is unique in that it operates its workshops with a small number of participants. However, it has been dormant since 2015.

Association of Korean Youth Diplomacy
(http://akyd.co.kr/)

The Association of Korean Youth Diplomacy or AKYD started as a Model UN conference in 2013 but turned into an organization in 2014. It wasn't initially hosted in Seoul but has been hosted in Seoul since its second conference. As an organization, AKYD has recruited partner schools so that could interact with each other. One of the benefits of being a member school of AKYD is that delegates participating in AKYD Model UN will be able to get discounted participation fees. However, AKYD too, seems to have become dormant since 2015.

GLIS (http://glismun.org/stoff2014/html/intro.html)

GLIS Model UN is one of the oldest Model UNs in Korea. It was started in 2010 by its current president In Gook Cho.

While GLIS Model UN used to be just a conference, it has started many projects over the past few years. In 2015, GLIS organized GLIS PRESS and GLIS VOLUNTEERS and has wrote a book about GLIS. Like AKYD, GLIS had also initiated a project to make alliances with partner schools.

Other Organization

 **Lead Korea**
(http://edu.chosun.com/leadkorea/)

MUNOS, the biggest and oldest Model UN conference in Korea, is hosted by Lead Korea, an organization under the Chosun Education. Model UN Leadership Summit and other conferences such as AYP are also hosted by Lead Korea. Lead Korea seems to have created its own ecosystem so that students who participate in activities organized by Lead Korea can continue participating in other activities Lead Korea provides. For instance, to become a secretariat or a chair in MUNOS, a student needs to participate in a set amount of activities provided by Lead Korea. Thus students who start with activities in Lead Korea aren't that easily seen in the other Model UN conferences in Korea. The interaction between people who participate in the activities Lead Korea provide and people who go to other Model UN conferences is rare compared to the interaction between people who only attend other conferences. To quote a student who had participated in four activities provided by Lead Korea, "It kind of becomes natural to continue participating in Lead Korea activities because all other students do that; there seems to be a gap between other conferences."

2013 MUNOS opening ceremony © 조선에듀케이션

2.2. Various Domestic Conferences

According to the Model UN Association of Korea (MUNAK) there are about 30 national Model UN conferences around Korea. In this section, I will try my best to group the conferences according to the difficulties they seem to have and talk about my experiences with some of them. I do understand that grouping conferences based on their difficulties is very subjective because difficulties change every year and can differ from committee to committee even in a single conference. That may be the reason why no one has published his/her opinion regarding this matter. However as I believe that there should be some materials rookie delegates or others should have to best choose which conference to participate in, I have organized conferences according to their difficulties based on my experiences. Once again, I do understand that this will most likely be subjective, but there also is a trend and a common viewpoint regarding some conferences whether they are difficult or not. I have written the list below based on my personal perspective but tried my best to be objective.

Difficulty Level ☆☆☆

GC: Seoul (Global Classrooms: Seoul) ☆☆☆

I attended the Security Council of GC: Seoul in 2014. Many experienced delegates came from all over Korea to participate. Delegates who received the Best Delegate award in this conference were granted an opportunity to participate in Global Classrooms International conference held in New York. GC: Seoul was very well organized by the secretariats and social events such as the 'GCian party' was held to enhance delegate experience at the conference. It is a conference I highly recommend.

To talk about my experience as a delegate, I applied to the Security Council because although I would not be able to win an award, I believed that it would be a great learning experience to interact with the top delegates in Korea. However as it turned out, everyone seemed to avoid registering for the Security Council due to its famous intensity and most top delegates went to the Advisory Panel Committee that has a double delegate system. Combined with this, the chair seemed to look more favorably upon the compromising aspect of Model UN rather than intense debates and as my style matched with that of the chair, I luckily won a Best Delegate award in the committee.

GC: International (Global Classrooms: International) ☆☆☆

GCIMUN is held in New York in the summer but has sub-conferences all around the world. Students who win Best Delegate awards in each region's respective conference get a chance to attend GCIMUN. Thus by winning the Best Delegate award in GC: Seoul, I was able to attend GCIMUN as a member of Korea's team.

A few weeks after GC: Seoul, I received an e-mail from the KICMUN secretariats who organized GC: Seoul and was notified of my placement in UNICEF: Congo and of other members of the team who would attend GCIMUN. A total of 10 students including me were on the list and while it was mostly comprised of high school students, there was one middle school student and one college student. Me and my partner should have met and researched the agenda to submit the position paper before the due

UNITED NATIONS ASSOCIATION
of the United States of America
A PROGRAM OF THE UNITED NATIONS FOUNDATION

May 09, 2014

Dear Sir or Madam:

Your student, **Sang yup Lee**, has been selected to participate as a member of delegation from *Global Classrooms*: Seoul representing the Congo at the **Global Classrooms: International Model UN Conference** on **May 15-18, 2014**.

Global Classrooms® is a program that provides educational opportunities to students in **urban public school districts** would not otherwise receive an opportunity to participate in Model UN. It is building young people's knowledge and confidence, and it is shaping the way students across the globe learn about the world around them.

This is the fifteenth year that UNA-USA is hosting this conference, with **1,500+ students attending from nearly 20 countries and over 15 states across America**. This three-day conference is held at the Grand Hyatt in New York and U.N. Headquarters, and gives students the opportunity to simulate the inner workings of organs of the United Nations (The conference website is available at www.gcimun.org). **The conferences' committees will be under the direction of some of the most qualified collegiate Model UN students across the world**. Selection to be a delegate at this conference is very competitive and Sang yup's long-time experience as in the *Global Classrooms* program makes him an invaluable asset to his team. Delegates are required to be in New York City on **May 15th** for Opening Ceremonies. I understand that this will conflict with the scheduled AP exam. I would be grateful if there is any way Sang yup could take the exam at a later time.

Please do not hesitate to email if you have any questions regarding Sang yup's participation at this conference, and I thank you in advance for your consideration in this matter.

Sincerely,

Juhi Kansra
United Nations Association of the USA
United Nations Foundation
Email: jkansra@unfoundation.org
www.gcimun.org

2014 GCIMUN invitation

date. However, both of us were in different boarding schools and we didn't submit the position paper by the due date. But we did research the agenda individually and finished the writing of the position paper during the 14 hour flight to New York and was submitted the position paper 2 days before the conference.

After putting down our luggage in the hotel, we had a tour of New York and started preparing for the conference that night. We were anxious because our guide who had attended the previous GCIMUN told us that there may be racism and it may be hard to get a chance to speak. Though I'm not 100% positive of the racism part, it was indeed harder to get a chance to speak because every delegate was eager to speak. Unlike typical Model UN conference in Korea which only 20~30% of students are active in each committee, the UNICEF committee in GCIMUN had about 80~90% of students who were very passionate. Another impediment during the conference was that I had to write draft-resolution by hand due to conference policy. However, I tried my best to use my time in New York sorely for the conference and eventually won an Honorable Mention with my partner.

Korea's team received its first Honorable Mention award in GCIMUN 2013 and we attained the second Honorable Mention award in GCIMUN 2014. Another group in Korea's team also won an Honorable Mention award that year and thus we had a total of two awards in 2014.

HARVARD WORLD MUN☆☆☆

Although Harvard World MUN is not a domestic conference, its 2015 conference was held in Seoul. And as I happened to participate, I'll talk about my experience about serving as its assistant chair. For background knowledge, Harvard World MUN is one of the largest international Model UN conferences with usually 2500 participants. HWMUN travels the world and is held in different countries every year. This year it was held in Seoul and next year it will be held in Rome. All the secretariat and chair positions are occupied by Harvard students and assistant chair positions are mostly occupied by MUNers in the region where the conference takes place. Out of 20~30 assistant chairs in HWMUN 2015, about 5~10 assistant chairs were from Korea.

HWMUN is for undergraduate and graduate students so technically high school students aren't eligible to participate other than by participating as its staff members. But when I submitted my application, I was told to take the interview and luckily I was able to serve as an assistant chair. Unlike domestic Model UN conferences where there are training sessions for deputy chairs, HWMUN seemed to select assistant chairs who already had the capability to work without training. The requirements for the document review on the first round were very intense-asking us to submit writing samples, our resumes, academic work, etc.

2015 Harvard World MUN opening ceremony

Before the actual conference, assistant chairs only had to write an update-paper (similar to chair reports but they served just like an update) and contact chairs to get a general understanding of the conference proceeding including grading rubrics. During the conference, we documented the flow of debate and moderated when the chair was busy. The role of an assistant chair in HWMUN seemed to have slightly less importance than deputy chairs in domestic conferences, but of slightly higher importance than rapporteurs.

Overall, the conference had a lenient atmosphere as compared to that of domestic Model UN conferences from including social nights with parties to ignite the 'World MUN atmosphere'. But the diversity of the conference was one I couldn't find in any other conferences and it seemed to have accumulated experience during the past several decades that served to enhance its professionalism.

2015 Harvard World MUN banner

2015 Harvard World MUN in session

세계 대학생 모의 유엔 대회인 '월드문 2015' 행사 참석 의장단이 15일 서울 한국외국어대학에서 핑거프린트 행사를 가진 뒤 호스트인 한국외국어대의 행사관계자들과 함께 기념촬영을 하고 있다. 한국외대와 하버드대가 공동 주최하는 이번 행사에는 전 세계 117개국 학생 2500여명이 참석하였다. 이와 관련한 기사가 당시 국내 여러 일간지에 보도되었다.
ⓒ 한국외국어대학교

2015 Harvard World MUN news article

MUNCCC (Model UN Climate Change Convention) ☆☆☆

I attended MUNCCC in 2013. This conference had many experienced delegates throughout the committees. Usually conferences with great awards like that of GC: Seoul has a deep pool of experienced delegates and because MUNCCC had a wide variety of awards ranging from Ministry Awards to University President Awards, there were a lot of experienced delegates who had already attended over 5 conferences. Delegates who received an award in this conference were granted a dinner at the British Embassy of Korea. One thing to keep in mind when attending this conference is that you should never pre-write a draft-resolution because MUNCCC strictly forbids it. MUNCCC is very strict with this policy and I've seen people being excluded from award considerations by pre-writing resolutions.

SIGMUN the LEGEND ☆☆☆

SIGMUN the LEGEND is a Model UN conference with a UNA-USA format that started in 2014. Though its history isn't long, this conference was made with the ideal to have the 'best delegates' from other conferences to participate in a single committee. Only students who had won an award in their previous conferences were allowed to participate; thus the quality of delegates was supreme in its 2014 conference. It is offered every summer as a one day conference and gave out premium awards such as the Georgetown University Award, UNDP Seoul Policy Center Award, Chungang University Award, etc.

YMUN: Korea (Yale Model UN: Korea) ☆☆☆

Unlike the three conferences mentioned above, I haven't attended YMUN: Korea. However, when I asked my peers about the difficulty in Model UN conferences, I heard that YMUN: Korea has a great pool of experienced delegates- many of whom that come from international schools in Korea. All the secretariats and chairs in this conference are students from Yale University.

Difficulty Level ☆☆

KMUN (Korea Model UN) ☆☆

Korea Model UN was the third Model UN conference I participated in as a delegate and my first Model UN conference which I participated in as a chair. While experiencing KMUN as a chair, I was able to see the secretariats devote significant time and effort to this conference. They prepared everything from A to Z and the chairs had off-line chair training every week for a total of 12 weeks. Korea Model UN has an image of prestige. This image comes from the well-preparedness of the secretariats that devote themselves to the conference. Thus, as the conference itself is well organized, a pool of experienced delegates comes to KMUN every year with the UNSC committee being the most advanced.

To talk more about my personal experience as a chair in KMUN, I applied to become a KMUN student officer (a term used in KMUN in place of a chair) because I heard that they had one of the most thorough chair training programs throughout Korea's Model UN conferences. Indeed we had to take the Rules of Procedure exam that had guessing penalties like the SAT I exam for 12 weeks and had to go through intensive chair training sessions. We also participated in making Model UN simulations for the delegate orientation. But overall, the secretariats genuinely cared for the student officers and provided us with foods in restaurants. It was a satisfying experience. Though it does need some amount of time commitment, I would recommend you to work as a student officer in KMUN if you are thinking of applying to a chair position.

YMUN (Yeonsei Model UN) ☆☆
SNUMUN (Seoul National University Model UN) ☆☆
Model IFRC (Model IFRC General Assembly) ☆☆

GLIS MUN ☆☆

GLIS Model UN has four different official languages and thus has different committees which are operated using four different languages. Though you can see some experienced delegates here, you will also see many rookie delegates. Conference difficulty seems to equate approximately with KIMC since I've received Best Delegate award in KIMC 2012 and in GLIS 6 (although as always, difficulties vary by years and by committees). The venue where GLIS Model UN is held at is expensive and thus the participant fee is expensive as compared to those of other student led conferences. Unlike some conferences which give out awards in a holistic manner, GLIS Model UN seems to strictly abide by the tally charts as one of its main awarding criterias; at least that had been the case when I participated in GLIS 6. GLIS Model UN has been working on a book about itself, so for more information about GLIS, it would be best to look at its publication.

Korea International Model Congress (KIMC) ☆ ☆

Delegates who usually participate in KIMC are high school students in the KIMC high school union. KIMC serves as a learning platform mostly for delegates participating in conference for the first time; however, there seem to be about 4~5 experienced delegates per committee. The conference fee is cheap compared to other conferences and KIMC has a unique meeting of all the committees at the end of the conference called the plenary session. In KIMC 2013, a total of three delegates were selected to receive premium awards at the plenary session and each received $1,000, $500, and a full scholarship to attend a leadership conference held in Australia. While the KIMC

왼쪽부터 추운주 중앙일보교육법인 대표, 구연우(경희대 총장상, 서울국제고2)양, 이성연(〃, 더킹스아카데미 고3)군, 임영진(중앙일보상, 경기외고1)양, 정진영 경희대 대외협력 부총장, 최선호(중앙일보상, 이화여고1)양, 송용원(멜버른대 리더십상, 서울국제학교 중3)양, 이상엽(〃, 글로벌선진학교 고1)군, 박한규 경희대 국제대학장.

중앙일보·경희대 주최 '한국 모의 국제회의'

제7회 한국 모의 국제회의(KIMC)가 지난 2~4일 경희대 법학관에서 열렸다. 중앙일보와 경희대가 주최하고, 주한 호주대사관과 호주 멜버른대가 후원했다. 참가자들은 중3~고3 학생들. 이들은 상·하원 등 미국 의회와 세계보건기구(WHO)·세계경제포럼(WEF) 등 유엔 국제기구들로 구성된 총 11개 위원회를 재연해 글로벌 이슈에 대해 토론하고 결의안과 법안을 작성했다. 모든 과정은 영어로 진행됐다.

총의장 김동주(예일여고3)양은 "참가자들이 대회 2주 전부터 모여 각 위원회의 의장단 회의를 시연하고 안건에 대해 세미나를 진행하는 등 회의 개최에 만전을 기했다"고 말했다. 심사위원장을 맡은 박한규 경희대 국제대학장은 "내용을 숙지하고 제한된 시간 내 자신의 의사를 제대로 전달할 수 있는지를 주로 봤다. 특히 주장이나 반박을 위해 객관적인 근거를 마련하고 설득력 있게 전달할 수 있는지를 평가했다"고 했다.

A news article on 2013 KIMC
in a daily newspaper 'Choonang Ilbo' on Aug. 5 2013

conference was sponsored by Joongang Ilbo Newspaper Company, the company had cut its relations with KIMC in 2014 and the Gyeonggi province has sponsored this conference since 2015.

KIMC is one of the few conferences in Korea that operates with a THIMUN format and its conference is divided into two areas: international and domestic. As the name Korea International Model Congress suggests, the domestic part of KIMC operates like a Model US Congress and the international part works like a typical Model UN conference. While attending KIMC 2012 and KIMC 2013, I had the feeling that KIMC places more emphasis on the debate related aspects. In KIMC 2012 I criticized others like debate competitions and received the Best Delegate award. In KIMC 2013 I backed up my arguments with intense research but didn't receive a committee award.

SIGMUN (Student International Government Model UN) ☆☆

SIGMUN is a student led conference held in Seoul. However what is unique about SIGMUN is that it has committees operating in both English and in Korean. Also, as SIGMUN was sponsored by Chungang University, Georgetown University, UNDP Seoul Policy Center, and by Best Delegate Institute in its 2014 conference, its participation fee was one of the cheapest in the nation. For a 3 day conference, SIGMUN charged only $130 if you applied early. I would like to recommend this conference for

뉴스	중앙대, 청소년 모의유엔대회 후원
대학교육	차현아 기자	chacha@unn.net

승인 2015.01.27 09:35:00

[한국대학신문 차현아 기자] 중앙대(총장 이용구)는 지난 24일부터 26일까지 흑석캠퍼스에서 청소년 모의유엔대회 'SIGMUN The Winter'를 후원했다고 밝혔다.

SIGMUN(Student International Governmental Model United Nations)은 중·고등학생에게 국제관계 시뮬레이션을 제공하는 모의유엔대회다. 이번에 열린 제2회 대회에는 150여명의 학생들이 참가했다. 유엔의 각국 대사 역할을 맡아 토론, 결의안 작성 등을 하며 협상과 발표능력을 함양하는 기회를 가졌다.

중앙대는 향후 국제기구로 진출하고자 하는 청소년들을 지원하는 의미로, 캠퍼스 공간과 식사, 우수 활동자에 대한 총장상 등을 지원했다.

SIGMUN의 사무총장을 맡고 있는 여의도고등학교 정성화 학생은 "국제사회와 정치 외교에 관심 있는 친구들과 함께 서로의 생각을 공유하는 계기를 마련하기 위해 기획한 행사였다. 흔쾌히 후원을 맡아주신 중앙대 관계자 여러분에게 감사드린다"고 전했다.

< 저작권자 © 한국대학신문 무단전재 및 재배포금지 >

A news article on 2015 SIGMUN
(http://news.unn.net/news/articleView.html?idxno=143916)

A committee photo in 2015 SIGMUN

A delegate making a speech in 2015 SIGMUN

rookie delegates and semi-experienced delegates to join (SIGMUN the LEGEND is also a conference hosted by the SIGMUN secretariats but is aimed at highly experienced delegates. While SIGMUN is annually held in winter, SIGMUN the LEGEND is annually held in summer; at least, this had been the decision made by the February of 2015).

HAISMUN (High schools Association of International Studies Model UN) ☆ ☆

HAIS MUN was held both in the summer and in winter at the Seoul National University GECE Center and its third conference was held in Kyung Hee University. It is operated with THIMUN style so even delegates who have never experienced Model UN before can easily adapt to the conference proceedings. Because HAIS MUN is a one day conference, it has the cheapest participation fee of $50. When I attended HAIS MUN the First, only about 3 delegates seemed to be experienced per committee- thus if you are ambivalent about doing Model UN, you might want to get a taste of Model UN here in its comforting atmosphere.

IMUN (Incheon Model United Nations) ☆ ☆
KHSMUN (Korea High School Model UN) ☆ ☆

📖 Difficulty Level ☆

JOINED MUN (JOINED Model UN) ☆
KAYMUN (Korea Advanced Youth Model UN) ☆
MUNNEO (Model UN New Equal Opportunity) ☆

CAMUN (Changwon Advanced Model UN) ☆

CAMUN is the one and only conference held in Changwon, a region next to Busan. Thus delegates who participate in this conference are mostly from Changwon and the conference only has committees that operate in Korean. Almost all participants are new to Model UN in this conference and the participation fee is one of the cheapest in the country. If you are uncomfortable with English but want to do Model UN for your first time, this would be the conference for you.

MUNIEVU (Model United Nations International Equality Vision Union) ☆
AKYD MUN (Association of Korean Youth for Diplomacy Model UN) ☆

MIMUN (Middle School International Model UN) ☆

There are many great conferences out there. However, if you are a middle school student, I definitely recommend you to participate in MIMUN which is hosted by students in the Hankuk Academy of Foreign Studies. This conference was my first Model

UN in 9th grade in 2012 and I learned a lot here. MIMUN is more like a Model UN workshop with continuous simulations. As most participants are new to Model UN, the chairs emphasize on explaining the Rules of Procedures as the conference proceeds. MIMUN may be a great start for you as it had been for me to start a Model UN career from middle school. (Note that almost every student wears their school uniforms at this conference; it was a bit embarrassing for me to be the only person wearing a suit in the committee).

There are many great conferences in Korea and I have selected some of the conferences I have experienced and heard of. A few years have passed since I participated in them so the information I provided above may have changed. I just hope that the reviews above can help you in the slightest sense to choose which conference to attend. To get a look of a complete list of various Model UN conferences in Korea, check out the last chapter in this book that serves like an appendix.

2.3. Market Trends

For the past few years, the Model UN market in Korea has slowly become overpopulated from having too many conferences. While Model UN conferences in 2011 could easily get 200~500 delegates, it is getting to the point where a conference having just over 100 delegates is considered a success. For instance,

MUNCCC used to have about 500~700 delegates but now has only about 200~300 delegates. GLIS MUN used to have about 200~300 delegates but now has only about 100 delegates (in GLIS X). Although there is a pool of a new generation of delegates getting into Korea's Model UN society, because too many conferences have been made for the past 2~3 years, each conference isn't getting enough delegates. Another reason that may explain this phenomenon is that all the conference schedules overlap with those of others. If the schedules don't overlap, having many conferences will not be much of a problem, but because conference schedule overlaps with those of others, especially during school breaks, some conferences had deficits and the secretariats had to make up for the loss of money (In a conference held in 2014, a group of participants cancelled their registrations altogether and the secretary general had to pay about $10,000 to make up for the loss).

Thus secretariats have tried different things to attract participants. Some conferences like CAMUN lowered its costs. Some conferences like HAIS MUN reduced the number of conference dates from 3 days to 1 day. Some conferences like SIGMUN the LEGEND tried to brand its prestige by only allowing qualified delegates to participate. Some conferences like SIGMUN attained sponsorships from various organizations to attract delegates with various awards from organizations like the Georgetown University, UNDP Policy Center, etc.

The problem still remains with the schedules of the

conferences. Since most Model UN conferences in Korea are held in January and between July and August, they overlap with each others. But because those months are the best times for students to participate in extracurricular activities, conferences aren't changing their schedules and so there inevitably is a consistent lack of participants for all conferences. There have been efforts to negotiate between different Model UN conferences in Korea to stop the overlapping of conference schedules. The Model UN Association of Korea (MUNAK) was made by some university students and me to perform that task. MUNAK had made a website and sent partnership e-mails to all conferences around Korea. However, because there weren't enough responses from conferences, the project to make a Model UN association in Korea has been stopped. A participation of the majority of Korea's Model UN conferences would be needed to ultimately solve this problem.

It would be nice if the United Nations Association: Republic of Korea (UNA-ROK) worked as the leading force to not only organize NMUN Korea for university students but also help high school students. If UNA-ROK acted as a 'plenary session' and other currently existing conferences as 'committees', the whole Model UN society in Korea may benefit. It may also be wonderful if UNA-ROK could work like UNA-USA that operates Global Classrooms conferences.

Chapter 3

Diverse Roles, Diverse Experiences

This chapter will try to help you understand the different roles that constitute Model UN. I will first start by talking about the roles of a secretariat and then the roles of a student officer (aka chairs), the roles of a delegate, and the roles of a staff.

2015 SIGMUN secretariats © 지주영

3.1. Secretariat

If you've just started your Model UN career, it may be hard to think of yourself in the position of the secretariats organizing the conference. I remember how 'godly' they looked on my first conference-thinking how in the world students like me could actually attempt to organize a conference! But with some experience in Model UN, it was possible for me to also organize one and it will be possible for you too.

But before moving any further, let's look at how secretariats are structured in typical conferences held in Korea.

Case A. This structure of secretariats is the typical organization for most conferences. Though there are some variations between them, the general structures can be applied to domestic conferences such as SIGMUN, GLIS MUN, MUNOS, HAIS MUN, and more.

A typical conference with about 120 participants will have the Executive Office of the Secretary General, Standing Advisor, Department of Financial Management, Department of Conference Management, and the Department of Technology.

Case B. International conferences such as Harvard World MUN and Yale MUN Korea have their secretariats dichotomized: there are two different Case A-structured secretariats. This is

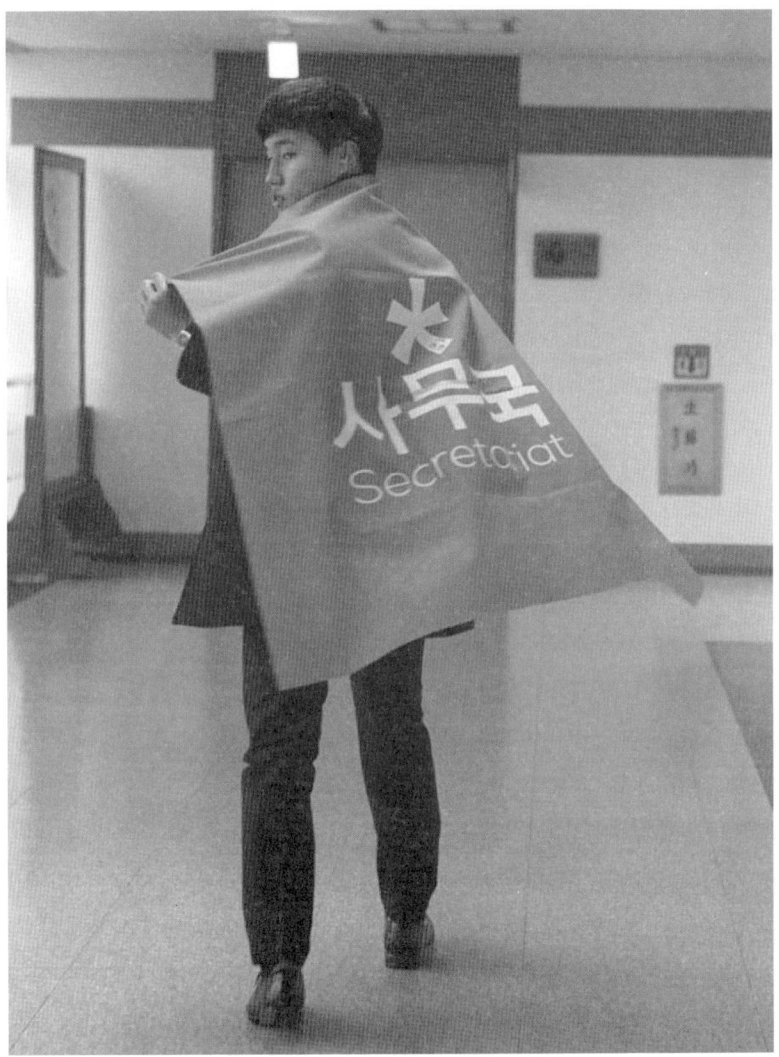
A secretariat with a secretariat banner

necessary since the organizing sector selects regional secretariats to accommodate the necessary regional mean where the conference is taking place.

Now that you have some vague sense of how secretariats are organized, I will discuss specific roles each department performs to prepare for the conference.

Department of Conference Management

If you have never worked as a secretariat before though you have had previous Model UN experiences, but don't have many technological skills like Photoshop and web-designing, you can start working in the department of conference management. (If you don't have Model UN experiences but do have skills that are required to fashion a conference by using Photoshop, web-designing, or other programs, you could work in the department of technology). Though its name varies among conferences, the department of conference management usually specializes in training chairs (student officers) and in making the Rules of Procedures along with making award criteria for the delegates. There may also be someone working on training staff members and providing general delegate services including the distribution of necessities like water to participating delegates; essentially, this department works to organize the logistics of the conference and thus will be a viable option for people who had a lot of experience in Model UN.

Chairs moderating a session

Department of Technology

This department is the one department where people with little or no Model UN experience can work in. Every conference needs a technician and if you are fluent with technology, you would be welcome in almost any conference. People in this department may manage simple tasks such as keeping a conference's Facebook page up-to-date to making a web page for the conference's advertisement. Press members for the conference may also be included in this department and make conference newspapers along with opening/closing videos. Usually only 1~3 secretariats are picked as technicians of a conference.

SIGMUN press center © 정혜인

SIGMUN press

Department of Financial Management

Finance is one of the most important aspects in organizing a conference. For a conference with 100 participants, a conference usually operates with 5,000,000 KRW. However, I've seen some cases where the money isn't used where it's supposed to be used when it isn't monitored. Though every conference should be registered with the tax administration of Korea for legal issues, not many conferences operating in Korea are actually registered. To my knowledge, every conference should be listed with the tax administration and pay taxes if the conference has some revenues. Thus to manage a conference's financial issues, a conference should enlist itself first with the government

Conference finance © GotCredit

and second, pay its taxes to keep its records clean. The department of financial management therefore should make budgetary measures before and after the conference to keep its account clean.

Standing Advisor

A standing adviser making a speech

Standing Advisors are those who have extensive knowledge or experience in running a conference and help the Executive Office of the Secretary General. There weren't Standing Advisors a few years prior to 2015 but are seen nowadays in many Model UN conferences. Some Standing Advisors I've met worked as emcees during closing ceremonies while some others worked to help the department of financial management to pay the taxes and keep the financial issues clear. Other Standing Advisors I know even acted as a Deputy Secretary General when a Deputy Secretary General couldn't work anymore for some reason. People usually aren't selected as Standing Advisors through an open recruit, but take the position when a Secretary General of a conference asks for help to work for the conference.

Executive Office of the Secretary General

The Executive Office of the Secretary General usually consists of 1 Secretary General and 2 Deputy Secretary Generals but some large conferences have several Secretary Generals and more Deputy Secretary Generals. This position too, though it may be recruited if a conference has an executive committee, is commonly occupied without an open recruitment process. Typically the Deputy Secretary General of the previous conference occupies the position of the Secretary General in the next conference and people from another department are selected as Deputy Secretary Generals. Essentially this office works as the spearhead of the conference and works to distribute tasks to each department and distributes works so that every member of the secretariat can perform to his/her full potential. This office also may do tasks such as registering hotels and busses along with making partnerships with other conferences and getting sponsors for the conference.

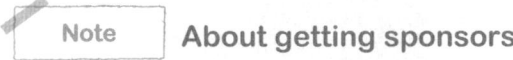 **About getting sponsors**

Though getting sponsorships may seem like a task high school students can't do, you would be surprised to see how many students actually get sponsorships from universities and UN related organizations while running a conference. If you can persuade the person in charge of giving sponsorships, it will not be hard to get one. You just need to persuade the person that by sponsoring your conference, the sponsor will get some kind of benefit in return. For university sponsorships, you may tell them that the university may advertise itself to prospective students participating in your conference. For UN related organizations, you may tell them that it will fit the UN related organization's ideals to help high school students learn about the UN through Model UN. Universities to provide classrooms to use and organizations provide awards or keynote speakers to a conference that had made sponsorship deals.

Sponsor speech by UNDP Seoul policy center at SIGMUN

Now I will specifically discuss the steps required to prepare for a conference. But before moving any further, I would like to state that you should work as a secretariat only after gaining enough experience in the field. Numerous Model UN conferences are sprouting up in Korea nowadays; but it also increasingly seems that the quality of conferences is being degraded. I've even seen someone organize a conference as a Secretary General in a conference held in Seoul after only two Model UN experiences (one experience as a delegate and one experience as a chair) and fail to fulfill the delegates' expectations by abruptly cancelling the conference. Another conference in 2014 had a Secretary General who never worked as a secretariat before and the conference resulted as a failure with huge debts. Though organizing a conference may not feel difficult if you actually try it, you shouldn't organize a conference without familiarizing yourself with the field. A conference needs mutual responsibility between secretariats and the delegates. However, if the secretariats running the conference don't have the knowledge and experience to provide a fruitful experience to its delegates, it would be better to not organize one in the first place.

 **to Organize a Conference from Scratch**

0. Before even thinking of starting a conference, you should question the reasons why you want to start one despite the existence of other conferences. Why are you attempting to do something that isn't necessary? If you are going to start a conference, are you willing as the Secretary General to risk paying for the loss if not enough participants are recruited? The three newly found conferences that operated in Seoul in 2014 had a loss of an estimated amount of 2,000,000 KRW each and it is highly likely that starting a new conference will result in some loss. Are you determined to take that risk? Are you determined enough to continue your work for about half a year despite your school work and tests? If you start a conference, you won't be the only one participating. Other secretariats will also be working for it and participants will trust your group to operate a conference and thus will be investing their fees into the conference budget. Looking at your circumstances, can you be responsible with the trust others put in you? Do you know what you are doing- what Model UN is about- comprehensibly? You should first ask yourself these questions and only if you are confident should you attempt to start a conference.
1. If you have decided to start a conference, you first need to think about where you would like the conference to take place. You need to consider already existing conferences in the region and how you would make your conference special;

remember the Model UN Trends section that was aforementioned in the previous chapter. With this in mind, you should recruit other secretariats to work with you for the next few months.

2. Things to consider when recruiting secretariats include their age, the schools they attend, the places they live, etc. No matter how much one has passion for the conference you are planning to make, if it takes 3 hours by train to go to the meeting place and if a potential secretariat is taking the Korean SAT this year and is attending a Korean public school, it will be extremely difficult for him/her to participate due to his/her predicament. Although the ability to work as an apt member of the secretariat is imperative, the applicant's situation shouldn't be ignored. The secretariats should join 5~6 months prior to the actual conference and it will be hard to continue for half a year for a secretariat without the right circumstances to work in. I'm not saying that those students shouldn't work as secretariats at all; but because I myself was in a similar situation and know how much time and effort I needed to put into the work, I'm saying that these factor shouldn't be considered lightly.

3. After recruiting secretariats, you need to decide whether to use the THIMUN procedure or the UNA-USA procedure mentioned in Chapter 1 of this book to run a conference. To reiterate, the general trend in Korea is to use the UNA-USA procedure due to its desirable aspect of flexibility although the THIMUN procedure is easier to work with for rookie

delegates. You will also need to choose the language which the committee will use. Korean committees, committees operated in Korean, are prominent in suburban and rural areas but are also becoming prominent in urban areas. After these decisions, determining which committees to operate, the date of the conference, and setting the length of the conference will be necessary. All the decision should work to support the ideology of why you are starting a conference despite the existence of other conferences and be based on recruiting participants in the area where your conference is taking place.

4. Now that the basics of your conference have been structured, you should distribute the tasks of delegate registration, conference advertisement, getting sponsors, homepage construction, delegate material purchases, and chair/staff selections/training…etc. between the members of the secretariats. Like any group project you have done in school, there may be some secretariats that slack off without clear tasks and it is thus your role to assign each member which tasks to work on. You should create a general plan regarding who-does-what-until-when and make business plans along with budget plans to get sponsorships. You also need to enlist your business with the tax administration of the region where you will have the conference. There are lots of things you need to oversee and thus selecting secretariats that have the faculty to passionately complete the work is imperative.

5. Chair recruits and staff recruits are essential factors that run a conference and thus should be recruited no later than two

months prior to the conference. It would be great if the chair registration opens before the delegate registration: about 2~4 months before the conference. The Rules of Procedure for the conference should be written by this time and materials such as chair scripts should be finished to be provided to the chairs during chair trainings. All sponsors should be contacted 2~3 months before the conference so that the details may be agreed upon a month prior to the conference.

6. When there are only two weeks left before the conference, every substantial preparation should have ideally been finished. Thus now, you can contact local newspaper companies to add news about your conference to their online newspapers and make reservations for food and water to be distributed during the conference. Specific schedules on how the conference will proceed should be posted on the conference website and the chairs should have finished their background guides (aka chair report) to be distributed to the delegates. Legal waiver forms should also be distributed to delegates through e-mail and delegate guides to the conference should be attached with it. If you have done all this 2 weeks before the conference, it means that you are on track.

7. You should have finished almost everything when there is only one week left before the conference. At D-7, secretariats should only need to prepare opening and closing ceremonies and fun events during the conference such as 'raffles' and 'superlatives'. In a conference I attended two years ago, the secretariats had a magic show and a buffet while other

conferences had the secretariats/chairs dancing to some K-Pop at the closing ceremony. Although Model UN is an academic experience, it should be fun! So try to make it fun. You can plan on creating a crisis during sessions with the chairs if you have some time.

8. Lastly, all secretariats, chairs, and the staff members should meet 1 day before the conference and rehearse how the conference will be run. All conference materials should be placed where they need to be placed and aspects regarding printing and award selections should be informed to the chairs. All aspects including microphone tests and projection tests should be conducted and the secretariat members should go around the conference settings to get a picture of where everything is located at. After all this, you will finally have finished preparing for the conference.

Note: During a conference there may be emergencies where some delegates are sick and cases where some delegates disappear at night. Therefore you should have basic medications prepared and have the staff/secretariats on night patrols in the conference venue. If none of the secretariats are adults, it is also good to have at least one adult stay with the conference to deal with emergencies or legal issues.

3.2. Student Officer

If the secretariats work to structure the conference, student officers are those who actually moderate it. Since student officers are the ones who spend the most time with the participants, the quality of the conference will be viewed based on how the student officers in each committee perform.

Most student officers I've met said that they usually began chairing after their 3rd or 4th delegate experience. With several experiences as a delegate and with weeks of training, working as a student officer isn't that difficult. You just need to know the rules for the specific conference, the general flow of debate, and some chair phrases which you can attain after being selected as a chair through chair training sessions.

Student officers moderating in a Model UN conference

If you want to work as a chair, you should first think about which conference you would like to chair in. This may be obvious but you should do so since every conference has different chair training styles. Korea Model UN for instance is known for its rigorous chair training of 12 weeks while MUNOS is known to have comparatively less training-according to a friend of mine who chaired in MUNOS. The Rules of Procedures for chairing are all slightly different between conferences so you may want to check the rules before applying as a chair. Also, note that while not all conferences make chairs pay to participate, some conferences have chairing fees that include hotel registration, food, and bus rides.

Most conferences have chair interviews and I've listed some typical interview questions below. Friends who had chair interviews told me that the questions below were almost the same as those that were presented to them during the interviews. The questions below may also prove to be helpful for you.

8 Steps | Chair Interview Questions

1. Why have you applied as a chair? Why to this particular conference?
2. How many experiences have you had with Model UN? What were they? How were they?
3. Which committee or agenda do you prefer the most? Why?

4. Which other conferences did you apply to as a chair and which conference would you focus on more if you are accepted as a chair to both conferences?
5. How many hours are you willing to spend on X conference's preparation per week?
6. In X situation, which rules should apply to our Rules of Procedures?
7. In X situation, how would you help the delegates?
8. (To UNSC applicants) How are UNSC rules different from the rules of other committees?

If you are selected as one of the chairs after the interview, you will have three responsibilities: memorizing the Rules of Procedures along with chair phrases, writing a chair report (background guide), and helping the delegates in your committee by answering questions about conference rules. As a chair you should know the rules better than any delegate and be fluent in moderating the committee as that's your primary role. I've attached a sample chair script below.

SIGMUN THE THIRD
Chair Script

1. Introduction

Committee, please come to order. Welcome to SIGMUN THE THIRD. The chairs would like to first introduce ourselves. My name is 000 and I'll be serving you as the head chair of the Historical Security Council/ United Nations Development Program. This is my deputy chair 000 and 000. Before moving into official session, the chair would like to clarify some rules in the committee. Use of electronic devices is strictly prohibited in the committee room unless given permission. If you need to use the restroom, please give your name tag to our administrative staffs before leaving the room.

2. Roll Call

Now we will proceed with roll call in alphabetical order. When the chair calls out your delegation, delegates may answer either present or present and voting. Please be reminded that delegates who answered present and voting may not abstain during substantive voting procedures. If the delegate next to you is late to the conference, please remind them to send a note to the chairs indicating whether they are present or present and voting.

With # delegates present, the committee has now met the quorum and will officially begin the first session. The committee is now open, and the chair would like to automatically set the agenda to agenda item A with chair's discretion, due to the fact that there is only one agenda debated upon in this committee.

Before moving onto the general speaker's list, are there any points or motions on the floor?

3. General Speakers' List

Are there any further points or motions in the committee?

Seeing none, the chair will now resume to the general speakers' list. Delegates wishing to be added upond the general speakers' list, please raise your placard high. Delegate A, B, C, you have been recognized in that order. Delegates who wish to be further added on the general speakers' list; please inform the chairs through note form. Delegate A, you have been recognized. Please approach the podium; you have 90 seconds to speak.

Delegate, you have # seconds remaining. How would like to yield your remaining time?

The delegate would like to yield to points of information. The delegate has opened himself/herself to # points of information. Are there any in the committee?

The delegate would like to yield to another delegate. That is in order. Delegate A, please go back to your seat.

Delegate B, please approach the podium.

The delegate would like to yield back to the chair. Thank you, delegate. Your time has now elapsed. Please go back to your seat.

The general speakers' list is now elapsed. Before moving on, are there any points or motions in the committee?

4. Points and Motions

Are there any further points or motions in the committee?

Motion to ex) move into a moderated caucus for the duration of # minutes, individual speaking time of # seconds, for the purpose of A. Are there any other motions or points in the committee? None. Seeing none, the committee will now move into voting procedure on the motion raised by the delegate of A. This is a procedural vote that requires a simple majority to pass.

Admin staffs please secure the doors and take your voting positions. Note passing will be temporarily suspended. All delegates wishing to vote for this motion, please raise your placards high.

Section one? #. Section two? #.

All delegates wishing to vote against this motion,

please raise your placards high.

Section one? #. Section two? #.

With # votes for and # votes against, this motion passes/fails.

Now the committee is in time for a moderated caucus for # minutes until ##:##. Delegates wishing to speak, please raise your placards high.

The time for the moderated caucus has now elapsed. Before moving onto the general speaker's list, are there any points or motions in the committee?

-

Are there any points or motions in the committee?

Motion to close the debate on agenda A. Are there any other motions or points in the committee? None. Seeing none, the chair will now entertain two speakers against this motion. Each speaker has 60 seconds to speak and yielding will not be in order. Are there delegate wishing to speak against this motion?

Now the committee will move into voting procedure on the motion raised by the delegate A. This is a procedural voting that requires a super majority to pass.

Admin staff, please secure the doors and take voting positions. Note passing will be temporarily suspended. All delegates wishing to vote for/against this motion, please raise your placard high.

-

Are there any points or motions in the committee?

Points of personal privilege. Yes delegate, please rise and state your point. This delegate believes that the room is too cold. That is in order, and you may be seated. Admin staffs, please adjust the temperature.

5. Resolution

Are there any further points or motions in the committee?

Motion to introduce a draft resolution. Are there any other motions or points in the committee? None. Seeing none, that is in order. As one of the sponsors of this draft resolution, please come up to the podium and read out the operative clauses.

Operative clause 1, operative clause 2, operative clause 3. Now the chair will entertain points of clarifications from the committee. All delegates that wish to raise points of clarifications please raise your placards high. Keep in mind that if a point of clarification is stated in an argumentative manner, the chair will have to rule out the point.

Would the delegate like to give an authorship speech?

Yes, this delegate would. Thank you delegate. The chair would now like to entertain points of information. Are there any in the committee?

No, this delegate would not. The chair highly encourages the delegates to make an authorship speech. If not, the chair would directly move into points of information. Are there any delegates who would like to ask points of information?

The draft resolution has now been formally introduced and delegate may now discuss this resolution.

6. Amendment

Are there any points or motions in the committee?

Motion to introduce an amendment. Are there any other points or motions in the committee? None. Seeing none, Delegate A please approach the podium. The chair will now read out the amendment that reads A.

The chair will entertain points of clarification. (not necessary for amendments to strike)

Would the delegate like to make an authorship speech?

Yes this delegate would. Thank you delegate. The chair would now like to entertain points of information. Are there any in the committee?

No, the delegates would not. The chair highly encourages the delegate to make an authorship speech. If not, the chair would directly move into pints of information. Are there any delegate that would like to ask points of information?

Now the amendment has been officially introduced and the chair will open up a limited speakers' list for the amendment.

English Committee Chair Script, Created by SIGMUN Secretariat
Content from-
SIGMUN THE WINTER / Standing Advisor, John Sang-Yup Lee
SIGMUN THE THIRD / Department of Conference Education, Serim Jang

Because I've only talked about the responsibilities of a chair, you may think of it as a role that is not exciting. But it is actually an interesting role. Unlike what you would have experienced as a delegate, chairs attain a different depth of knowledge while writing a chair report and a different perspective that comes from staying as a third party during debates. Also since chairs often meet to train, relationships between chairs tend to be deeper than those of delegates. Although I personally prefer debating as a delegate during sessions, I've chaired twice and experiencing Model UN in a new fashion was worth the time and effort.

3.3. Staff

Staff members occupy a crucial role in Model UN. They connect secretariats with chairs and chairs with delegates. Without staff members volunteering to work as the hands and feet of the

A staff meeting at night

Staffs leading the delegates to the conference venue

Staffs contacting each other

conference, the secretariats wouldn't be able to run it. But there exist some delegates and even some members of the secretariats/chairs who views the volunteers as if they are superior to them. And when there is this atmosphere, volunteers no longer feel motivated to help and spend their time at a conference. I staffed at some conferences and when I felt this atmosphere, it really didn't make me want to participate. To combat this problem, some conferences such as MUNNEO picked 'security' instead of 'staff' and selected security personnel with other members of the secretariats to try to have an equal standing by eradicating subtle discrimination.

Despite the possibility of subtle discrimination, I believe that working as a staff member is an experience one may have for his/her benefit especially at one's first Model UN conference. If you are new to Model UN and don't want to participate as a delegate, you could apply as a staff member and see how Model UN functions. Some students apply as observers for their first conference and that is great; however, I would recommend interested students to apply as staff members because not many conferences in Korea have great observer programs and observers usually just sit in the back watching delegates debate. The best way to participate in your first conference is to apply as a delegate, but if that's too intimidating, apply as a staff member.

If you apply as a staff and become accepted, you will be trained to lead the delegates to designated areas during certain circumstances such as lunch and will learn basic Rules of

Procedures to get to know the flow of the conference and be expected to act accordingly during voting procedures.

3.4. Delegate

> "Delegates are the protagonists of Model UN. They fulfill the main purpose of Model UN through forming caucuses and writing resolutions. Model UN is a stage for their performances."

Working as a secretariat is exciting, working as a chair is fun, and working as a staff is interesting. But above all, performing as a delegate has always been the most exciting part of Model UN for me. I love the feeling of meeting new people in my committee during the opening ceremony and introducing my ideas (my country's ideas to be precise) to the floor-booming my voice into the microphone. At first I had butterflies in my stomach every time I tried to speak and so I didn't know that I would indulge myself to the world of Model UN this much. I never knew I could find joy in Model UN by acting as a delegate when I first heard of it. Only by experiencing Model UN first-hand as a delegate was I able to fully appreciate it.

You do not need any prerequisites to register as a delegate. Although most conferences make you to write down your previous Model UN experiences, it's okay to have no prior experience. Although having a lack of previous Model UN experiences may sometimes inhibit you from representing major countries such as the US or China, you still will be able to register without any problems. But as a delegate, you will be expected to know your country's stance and have several solutions to tackle the issue mentioned in the agenda. It is also your role to speak up and make use of the time during sessions. For the three days of a Model UN conference, some delegates speak once or none while others speak hundreds of times. What you attain from Model UN is gained by how much actively you participate. Though it is unlikely that you will be recognized as a great MUNer at your first conference, if you try hard to prepare and memorize the rules, you will be recognized with awards in your future conferences. (I've devoted the entire next chapter to the responsibilities of a delegate and tips to becoming best delegates so check it out if you're interested).

Being a delegate in Model UN is also exciting disregarding any content related matters. By participating in Model UN, you get to meet your peers who have similar interests. Most people I met during Model UN were generally interested in international relations and had similar interests as myself; we were able to quickly become friends together. We were also able to go beyond Model UN to work on other activities such as working in a youth committee of the Korea government as we shared the activities we did outside of Model UN. The ties formed in Model UN allowed us to have a wider range of view on which activities to pursue and ultimately led to advancements beyond Model UN. Model UN essentially gave us valuable connections that we wouldn't have formed otherwise.

A delegate speaking during moderated caucus

Delegates after the conference

A delegate's birthday cake during a conference

Committee photo © 지주영

A dinner after the conference

Chapter 4
How to Be a 'Best Delegate'

Out of my 20 Model UN experiences, I won awards at 7 out of the 10 conferences I've attended as a delegate. Awards aren't everything in Model UN. Model UN is much more than just hunting down awards. However, awards are one of the aspects that motivate delegates to strive harder and thus I've dedicated this chapter to explain how to prepare to become a best delegate.

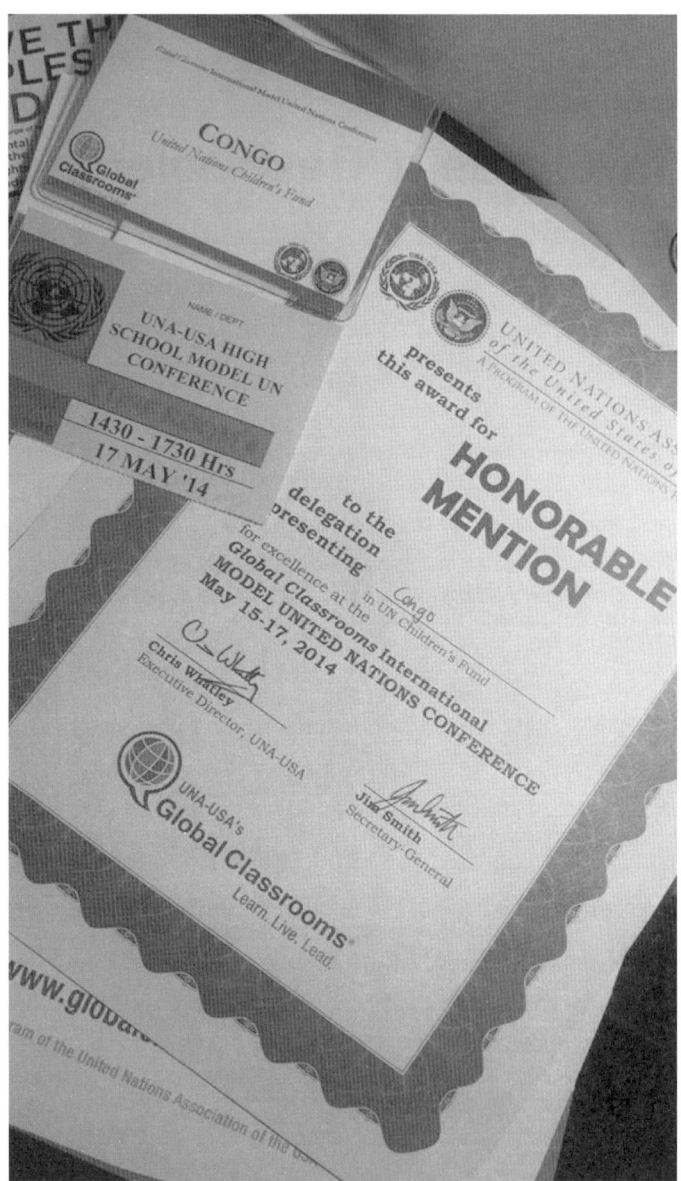

The award I received in 2014 GCIMUN

4.1. Research, Research, and Research

The first thing to do to become an apt delegate is to research thoroughly. You should know your country's stance on the agenda and your country's past, current, and future solutions that supports it. You also need to learn the UN's past and current actions on the issue and general trends of other country's policies. Though researching other countries' policies and stances may feel like a waste of time, if you know them, you will be able to decide which countries to work with and will be able to refute a country that's not speaking according to its stance.

Personally when I do my research, I google different key words of my agenda several ways. Then I click all the results that come

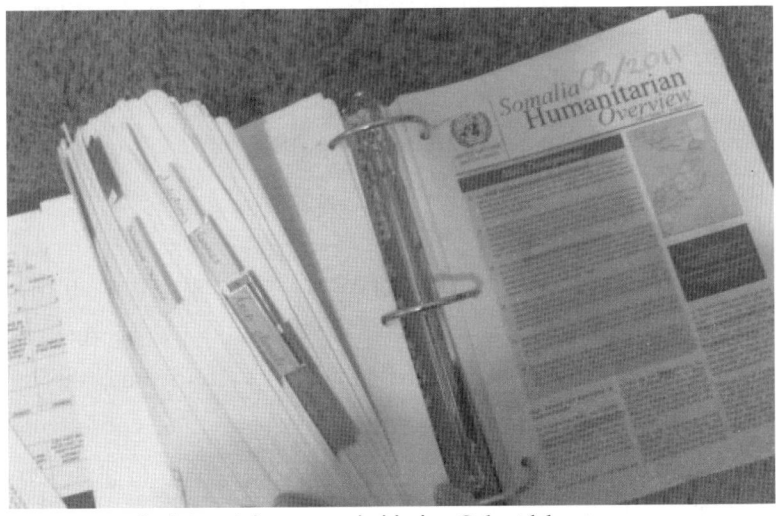

A delegate's research binder © bestdelegate.com

out on first page, paste them into word document if needed, and print them to read. I usually have about 200~300 A4-sized pages and I skim through them while highlighting information I can utilize during the conference. For me this process takes about 8~10 hours and I do it about two weeks before the conference. After finishing reading 200~300 pages of information from various sources including thesis papers, UN reports, news articles, chair reports from other Model UN conferences with the same topic, etc. I will have attained general ideas of the topic; actually I will have enough information to attend small conferences that aren't very competitive. Since most position papers are due a week before the conference, I write down my position paper after my general research to condense my highlights into 2~3 pages. This process seemed to internalize the information from my brain into my heart so that I can speak it during the sessions. I always think about ways to utilize highlighted information when highlighting it and practice using it. I believe that this process has always been crucial in making the material become my own and allowed me to flexibly use it according to the situation I'm in during the sessions.

If I have a week left after this process, I usually look up other country's stances by reading news articles and by asking other delegates about their positions if I happen to find them through Facebook or happen to know them from previous conferences. I also contact the chair to understand his/her chairing styles and the conference award criteria. I jot down all the possible solutions to the agenda in accordance with my country's stance and search for more documents to support the solutions I am constructing to refute any rebuttals. The only spear and shield you have in a conference is your substantiated information so it's best to gather and digest all the information you can before the conference.

About jotting down possible solutions before the conference, you should be aware of conference policies regarding pre-written resolutions. Conferences such as Model UN Climate Change Convention (MUNCCC) don't allow pre-written resolutions and so your solutions shouldn't be in a resolution format when attending this conference. Note that this doesn't mean that you shouldn't have your solutions; it means that you need to have solutions before the conference but shouldn't have them in a resolution format. But if a conference does allow pre-written resolutions, it would be best for you to write a pre-written resolution with all the pre-ambulatory clauses and the operative clauses formatted to match the conference guidelines. This is imperative because other delegates will follow the delegate who seems to know what he/she is doing and one of the best ways to show this is by having a draft-resolution on hand. Though national power determines who the leader is in the real UN, in Model UN, the nation that knows the most becomes the leader.

When I make my draft-resolution, I usually have 7~8 strong operative clauses and bring 10 copies (depends on the size of the committee I'm in) to share with other delegates. Just be reminded that you should prepare your solutions after asking a secretariat member or a chair whether it would be okay to have them in a resolution format before the conference. Also, be reminded that you having a draft-resolution all set shouldn't mean that you won't be accepting ideas of other delegates. I'll talk about this later but Model UN is about cooperation and though it is nice to have your ideas laid out before others, other ideas shouldn't be eschewed.

Research is everything you can do to prepare yourself. If you have finished your research, there are several other things you can do to advance your research. A few years ago, I printed out the UN Charter to memorize some phrases and I've learned that some essential phrases come in handy to illustrate my point in some cases. For instance, the UN Charter Article 2 Section 7 states that "Noting contained in the present Charter shall authorize the United Nations to intervene in matters which are essentially within the domestic jurisdiction of any state...." and I was able to quote this phrase in numerous conferences, especially in the Security Council. Last year, I met someone who actually called his country's embassy to validate his stance and obviously everyone was impressed with his research. It would be obvious to say that this added credibility to his statements.

There are delegates that do win awards without much preparation. They rely on their fluency in English and skills of public speaking. However, without research, a person can only go so far. If there is just one delegate in a committee that had

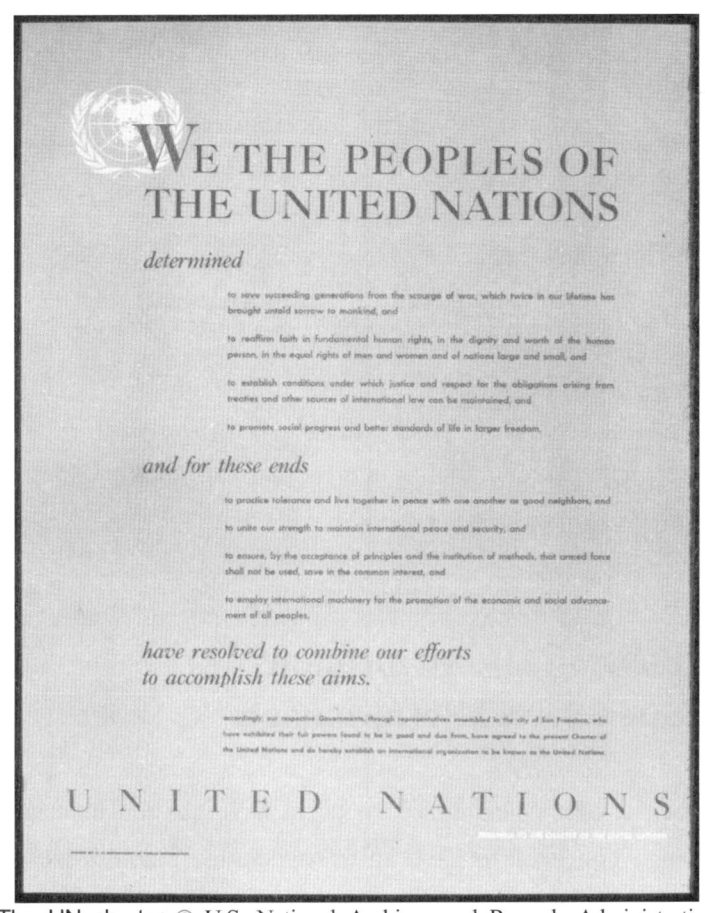

The UN charter © U.S. National Archives and Records Administration

researched thoroughly, then although a delegate may flaunt his speaking skills, the chairs will pick whoever is more knowledgeable. Flaunting your research through making research binders and putting them on your desk with a loud THUMP would be better than flaunting your speaking skills that don't

Chapter 4. How to Be a 'Best Delegate' | 117

necessarily bring substantive matters to the floor.

Below are links that may help your research
1. UN Charter (http://www.un.org/en/documents/charter/)
2. UN News Centre (http://www.un.org/News/)
3. UN Document Database (unbisnet.un.org)
4. Model UN Research Guide by Best Delegate
   (http://bestdelegate.com/research/)
5. CIA World Factbook
   (https://www.cia.gov/library/publications/the-world-factbook/)
6. Model UN Association of Korea Q&A forums
   (http://cafe.naver.com/theworldwithus)

4.2. Passion Shown through Speech and Performance

To be the best delegate, you need to have passion in what you are doing. You need to have an overwhelming passion that flows out of you so that every move you make seems to be made with confidence. Every speech you make should have your soul in it and every stride you take toward the podium should be flowing with enthusiasm. The butterflies in your stomach will exist but they should essentially feel like some kind of anticipation that exciting things are about to happen. Speaking in front of others shouldn't be a burden; rather, it should instead feel like a platform upon which you can flaunt the effort you have made for preparation. When you feel these things, it will mean that you find Model UN fun because it is exciting for you. You will want to participate in Model UN because it is fun and the excitement will make you stand out in front of others. By finding passion in Model UN, your passion will lead you to your success.

About 4 years ago, I indulged myself in learning the art of public speaking. I don't exactly know the reason why I was enamored with public speaking, but I found debate competition videos from the YTN & HUFS Youth English Debating Championship finals fascinating. Wanting to acquire the art of public speaking myself, I've searched for famous public speaking videos from YouTube and tried to mimic their styles and articulate my own. Wanting to be great at public speaking, I've

A passionate speech attracts attention

turned on debate competition videos while sleeping in hopes of subconsciously absorbing their styles (though I don't know if it actually helped or not). After several months of mimicking great debaters and speakers, I was able to see myself improve and prepared myself to attend a debate contest. Although I couldn't participate due to not having debate partners to work with, the skills I attained during the 4 months helped enhance my public speaking skills in Model UN. I didn't suddenly become a master of public speaking. But I was able to gain confidence in it. Also during my Model UN career, I sometimes made and wore costumes of my assigned country and even tried to make stomping noises while approaching the podium in order to demonstrate confidence. When I reflect on these actions, I feel that they were a bit childish but I did it because Model UN felt

Performance on stage © Andrew E. Larsen

like a theater for me with me being the leading actor. Those actions were marks of my enthusiasm. Had I not loved various aspects of Model UN on speaking opportunities and acts of a delegate, I wouldn't have devoted this much time and wouldn't have achieved much. By participating in Model UN with enthusiasm, by having passion for Model UN, I could indulge myself in the field and get the most out of it. Your passion will help you become a best delegate.

4.3. Model UNITED Nations

Model UN conferences are not debate competitions. I'm reiterating this fact because students who have done debate previously act as if Model UN is another platform for debate competitions and shuts out others' opinions as being illogical. While that might have been necessary for debate competitions where the oppositions' opinions should only be rebutted, Model UN doesn't quite work like that. Yes there are debates between delegates. But this activity should focus more on making constructive solutions rather than disparaging other's opinions.

Some delegates may assert that they have received awards in the past even when they acted as a debater instead of being a negotiator in a conference held in Korea. Yes it was possible to become a Best Delegate awardee three years ago even if a delegate acted as the Best Debater; however, it has become increasingly harder for debaters to becomes Best Delegate awardees as the chairs in Korean Model UN conferences are starting to realize that Model UN isn't just about who is right and who is wrong. In this changed trend, I've seen previous debaters attend 4 conferences in a row aiming for awards to no avail. Model UN is Model UNITED Nations after all. This trend is also noticeable if you look at how the Rules of Procedures have changed over the last 2 years. While there were rules about main-submitters 2~4 years ago, most conferences nowadays instead have sponsors so to emphasize a collaboration of efforts.

Thus to become true best delegates, you shouldn't act as a power delegate who dictates his/her own way throughout the conference. To become a best delegate, you need to have your

Model UNITED nations © 지주영

position and your dogma set to have your country's principle prevail. But you should also leave some space for cooperation. To become a best delegate, you should be a leader of your committee by bringing out the best of other delegates to merge everyone's efforts into your resolution.

When everyone surrounds you during an unmoderated caucus, you may want to tell people in the circle to open it up a little so to have others in the back also have their voices heard. When writing resolutions, you could divide the tasks on writing operative clauses in your resolution to have someone work on

Delegates writing resolutions

foreign policy, someone on domestic solutions, and another group to work on regional policies. Using this teamwork, your resolution should consist of every member's rich ideas that could better support your country's principles.

4.4. Position Paper, Resolution, Amendment

If you have researched a lot and are enthusiastic about working with others, you will now only need to write down what you have in your mind to share with others. Here I will talk about some tips I've learned from the past several years in utilizing the three types of papers.

1. Position Papers. Position papers are papers that are used by chairs to see how much preparation a delegate had done before the conference. They are usually due a week before the conference and if you do not submit a position paper, you will likely not be considered as an awardee from the start of the session. So in other words, to stand out even before the conference you should write a great position paper that can impress your chairs. Unlike international conferences, there usually aren't position paper awards in Korea. But a strong position paper will still work for your benefit. A typical position paper should be 2~3 pages long and talk about 1. Brief history of the issue and UN's past actions, 2. Your

country's stance and its rationale consisting of an illustration of past and current actions, and 3. Your future solutions to the problem.

When writing position papers, be reminded that you should have citations at the end of your paper because some chairs may be offended to find a document not referenced. You might also want to have a cover page for your position paper that consists of the symbol of your country and the address of your embassy to grab the chair's attention.

Below is a position paper my partner and I wrote for the Global Classroom: International Conference.

Global Classrooms International Model United Nations
Republic of Congo
Permanent representatives to the United Nations 201 East 42nd street, suite 405
New York, NY 10017
Tel) (201) 557-5001 Fax (201) 557-5009

Gender equality is a fundamental human right which every single individual should recognize and acknowledge. And by tackling an issue of child marriage, we can make a significant contribution to the elimination of human rights abuses. Indeed, child marriage is recognized as one of the most fatal social ills that imposes extreme threats on maternal health, human dignity and education opportunities of children.

Although the development in various aspects throughout this 21st century has made a notable progress in abolishing the child marriage around the world, only few are benefiting from such advancement. Obstacles such as poverty and restricted cultural perceptions serve as the prominent causes that instigate child marriage in first place. As a consequence of such deficiency or cultural beliefs, nations suffer from serious domestic violence issues, high infant mortality rate, HIV/ AIDS and delayed economic growth in long term.

Around the world, about 10 million girls are married every year before they reach the age of 18. In the developing nations, 1 in 7 girls is married before her 15th birthday, with some child brides as young as 8 or 9. Regionally, 46% of girls under 18 are married in sub-Saharan Africa, 21% in the Caribbean, and 18% in the Middle East. In addition, studies have shown that one in nine girls, or 15 million, have been forced into marriage between 10 to 14. In Congo, it was discovered that only 33% of 20-24 year old females are married by the age of 18. In other words, more than 60% of the female populations are forced into child marriage despite a clear legislation prohibiting the marriage before 18.

Child marriage occurs when parents arrange the marriage without consent of the fully informed girl. For most of the families, poverty is one of the major reasons that they decide to send the girls away. Because there is a limited amount of food and resources available, girls often remain as a burden of responsibility to the poor family. On the other hand, if the girls are sent to their husbands' houses, it would simply decrease the responsibility for the family by having one less mouth to feed, one less kid to take care of. In addition, by marrying off their daughters, parents can even earn a large amount of money or livestock as a form of price paid for their daughters. Unfortunately, the younger the children, the less power they have to speak against the arranged marriages. Therefore, young females are subjected as the most vulnerable victims in child marriage. Another reason that young women are exploited for child marriage is due to the high potential fertility. A girl who is married off at the age of 14 is guaranteed to have more children than a girl who starts having children at the age of 24. And because daughters' parents are obliged to pay more dowry when the girl is young (since they are handing the responsibility over to the husband's family), from the adults' perspectives, it is the best to marry off the girls at young age- since it ensures daughter's family to save money while it enables the husband's family to obtain more children.

Not only poverty, but cultural perception and social norm within the community are also a prominent stimulant for child marriage. In developing nations, it is believed that the girls honor their families through their deeds. It is considered an extreme disgrace to the family if the girl ends up having sexual intercourse with a male before the marriage; thus, the parents determine that the best way to avoid such embarrassment is to arrange a marriage when the kids are young. Surprisingly, it has been reported that a lot of parents do not even hesitate from believing the early marriage as the best mechanism to protect their daughters from sexual violence.

Unfortunately, early marriage does not assure protection of children at all; rather, it puts girls at the risk of severe violence. Girls are often forced into exhaustive house labor, required to fulfill their responsibility as adequate mothers and wives. Also, they are exposed to the greater danger of physical and sexual violence that end up imposing physical and psychological harms upon them. Particularly, because the girls often do not have enough sexual experiences before they marry their husbands, they have higher chances of catching sexual diseases such as HIV/AIDS- which leads to higher rate of infant mortality (as the babies are born from immature bodies). Aside from disparate health issues, child brides could be subjected to eve teasing and acid throwing if they are married to their low dowry.

There had been various attempts and efforts to combat

child marriage internationally. One of the most effective, beneficial, feasible and practical way to decrease the rate of child marriage is education. The United Nations and other organs around the world had first feasibly dealt with the issues regarding child marriage since 2013. Acknowledging child marriage as a clear violation of human rights that usually deprives innocent girls of education and freedom; we had tried to make guidelines to resolve child marriage using the frameworks of previous principles like the 1948 Universal Declaration of Human Rights (UDHR), Convention on the Elimination of all Forms of Discrimination against Women (CEDAW), and the Convention on the Rights of Child (CRC). However as the United Nations should comply with its charter's article 2 section 7 which talks about a nations' sovereignty, it had been hard to promote solutions that can also alter one nation's cultural norms and traditions. But as each individual government also saw child marriage as a problem which limits their nations' growth, most nations had issued laws like the Dowry Prohibition Act which prevents the killing of women. The Republic of Congo had issued the laws and legislation to protect children and had made the minimum marriage age set at the age of 18. But progress hadn't been made much because nations lacked the infrastructure to promote the legislations comprehensively.

Republic of Congo had been attempting to engage in elimination of gender inequality in developing nations and paid special attention to this issue. At the end of the day, the most important aspect of the committee is to raise international community's willingness to actively support the development by seeking for an economical but effective education distribution policy, along with the fixation of cultural bias upon young female children. After all, nations will be able to promise sustainable mechanism that will ultimately decrease the rate of child marriage.

The delegation of Congo would like propose that we feel the responsibility and commitment to participate in solving this problem. We are currently considering implementing the policies that establishes the foundation for eradication of child marriage. For example, in order to increase accessibility to education, we can utilize the technology; by providing cheap, second- hand laptops (e-wastes) to children in LEDCs, we can certainly increase accessibility and sustainability of education. Moreover, some other solutions will have to tackle the issues of societal stereotypes and biased cultural norms. Indeed, we are looking forward to have discussion and listen to other nations' ideas as well and overall, Republic of Congo is hoping to approach to the new goals and solutions that are beneficial, feasible, practical and effective in terms of solving the problems. Once again, we would like to emphasize the significance of other nations' positions and support on this issue as education is what determines our future.

Finally, Republic of Congo would like to this position paper with the following quote by a current Secretary-General of the United Nations, Ki Moon Ban

"Child marriage is a violation of human rights. By 2020, 142 million innocent young girls worldwide will be separated from their friends and family, deprived of an education and put in harm's way because of child marriage. Together, let us resolve to end the discrimination and poverty that perpetuate this harmful practice. And let us help those who are already married to lead more fulfilling lived. All members of society will benefit when we let girls be girls, not brides."

Thank you.

2. Resolutions. As mentioned previously, your resolution should be comprehensive with many nations' ideas while making the general direction of the resolution to serve your country's purpose. A resolution should typically have about 7~8 operative clauses and its pre-ambulatory clauses should exist

to mention the problems that need to be reminded and the operative clauses should exist to propose the solutions to the problems; so it would be good to coordinate each pre-ambulatory clause with operative clauses and draft a resolution in that order. To write a good resolution, you will need to think comprehensibly. Some questions you may want to answer may include: How can local communities act? How can regional organizations act? How can different nations collaborate? How can international organizations work? Along with these inquires, you should definitely address the questions mentioned in the chair report since that's what your chair explicitly wanted you to answer. Also if you want to discuss your resolution with others more openly, you can submit your draft-resolution as a working paper first and after everyone agrees upon its content you can turn it in as a draft resolution and put it on a vote. Because official draft resolutions need to be amended with formalities in order to be changed, it is very time-efficient to debate on a draft-resolution in the form of a working paper. Another tip to utilize when writing your resolution is to break up its contents. This is to prevent your clause from being stuck just because some delegates believe that a word should be deleted. If you have your main operative clause and sub clauses along with sub-sub clauses, it would increase your chances to keep your main clause intact through the sacrifice of some sub or sub-sub clauses. Along these in mind, you should read a conference's Rules of Procedures thoroughly to see if there are any mention about a motion to change the order of voting resolutions. Since some conferences allow only one resolution to pass, if there is a motion to change the order of voting for the resolution, you may utilize it to your advantage. Lastly, remember that when writing a resolution, you should never interfere with a nation's sovereignty and refrain from mentioning specific statistics. Your solutions should be clear without going against UN ideals. Remember that you are a representative of a nation and thus you are only setting the general guideline on which experts of different fields will work with later. Writing a draft resolution at first may feel awkward. But if you practice 2~3 times, you will get the hang of it.

Below are a sample resolution and some perambulatory/ operative clauses.

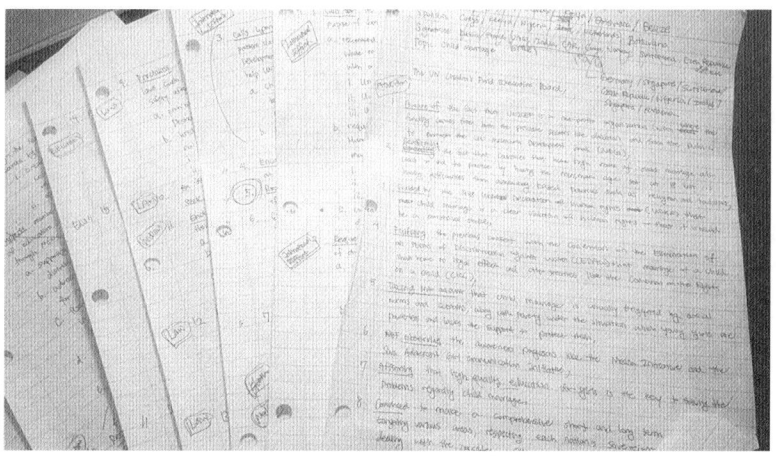

My resolutions from 2014 GCIMUN

Sample Opening Pre-ambulatory Clauses	Sample Opening Operative Clauses
Affirming	Accepts
Alarmed by	Affirms
Approving	Asks
Award of	Authorizes
Bearing in mind	Calls for
Believing	Calls upon
Confident of/that	Condemns (Security Council only)
Convinced that/by	Confirms
Declaring	Congratulates
Deeply concerned	Considers
Deeply disturbed	Decides
Deeply regretting	Emphasizes
Desiring	Encourages
Emphasizing	Endorses
Expecting	Hopes
Expressing its appreciation/satisfaction	Invites
Further deploring	Notes
Guided by	Proclaims
Having considered	Reaffirms
Having examined	Recommends
Keeping in mind	Requests
Noting with regret	Sanctions (Security Council only)
Nothing further	Supports
Reaffirming	Suggests
Realizing	Takes note of
Recalling	Trusts
Taking into account	Urges
Taking note of	
Viewing with Appreciation	
Welcoming	

 **Resolution**

Committee: United Nations Security Council
Question of: Situation in the DPRK: Non Proliferation
Submitted by: People's Republic of China

United Nations Security Council,

<u>Fully alarmed</u> by the fact that talks between nations about the situation in the DPRK hadn't been discussed multilaterally since 2009,

<u>Fully aware</u> of the fact that multilateral talks had been halted due to some nation's stance to talk with having pre-conditions,

<u>Considering</u> the DPRK's unstable political power structure with the Kim Jung Eun regime,

<u>Deeply concerned</u> with vast amount of citizens in the DPRK under the poverty line due to its economy,

<u>Taking into consideration</u> the fact that resolution 1718 and resolution 1874 along with resolution 2087 and resolution 2094 had been about sanctioning the DPRK which didn't bring about fruitful results,

<u>Having regarded</u> the essential need to implement NPT worldwide and the need to implement the failed Joint Declaration on the Denuclearization of the Korean Peninsula,

<u>Deeply disturbed</u> with the fact that while the DPRK possesses over 5,000 tons of chemical and biological weapons it had

not signed the CWCs and BTWCs along with the Geneva protocol,

Emphasizing the intricate position China has on this issue and believing its role to be important in solving the crisis,

Recognizing the recent national position change of nations known to have close relationship with the DPRK such as Iran and Libya,

1. *Affirms* the need to talk about the enforcement of the Nuclear Non-Proliferation Treaty (NPT) to all member states in the United Nations for the purpose of international peace and security in the 2015 NPT review conference with the conditions such as but not limited to:
   a. endorsing member nations in the UN to sign the NPT having considered their consent,
   b. calls upon the IAEA to investigate UN member states' nuclear facilities with the following conditions:
      i. considering the consent made by each nation,
      ii. considering each nation's situations made in further Security Council meetings,
   c. condemning nations that do not abide by the NPT with having the following prerequisites:
      i. discussing each nation's situations to be decided upon further Security Council meetings,
      ii. acknowledging the fact that international nuclear non-proliferation is imperative by the form of calling upon nations to sign the NPT;
2. *Emphasizes* the need for complete denuclearization of the

Korean Peninsula with conditions such as but not limited to:

a. fully recommending the implementation of the Joint Declaration on the Denuclearization of the Korean Peninsula which had failed in 1991 due to the remaining nuclear arsenals in Korea,

b. acknowledging the fact that the DPRK had withdrawn from the Agreed Framework bilaterally made with the US after the fail of implementation of the Joint Declaration,

c. condemning nations that go against UN Charter Article 2 Section 7 regarding a nation's sovereignty to decide for itself whether to disarm nuclear arsenals within its nation,

d. appealing the need to affirm the complete denuclearization by the IAEA,

e. complete denuclearization of the Korean Peninsula being met by 2018;

3. *Proclaims* the need to economically stabilize the DPRK for the purpose of ensuring basic human rights such as clothes/food/and shelter by means such as but not limited to:

a. promoting further trade between the DPRK and nations within its proximity by using the appropriate amount from the UN general budget to facilitate trade more effectively with having conditions such as but not limited to:

i. the amount of the budget being discussed in the General Assembly after the DPRK conducts multilateral talks between nations in its proximity for the purpose of deciding the budget's needed amount,

ii. nations in the DPRK's proximity being decided by the nation of the DPRK,

iii. facilitating trade by using means such as but not limited to building a trans-Asian train route that had stopped after the stopping of the six party talks,

b. promoting humanitarian aid to be sent to the citizens of the DPRK using means and considering situations such as but not limited to:

i. conducting advertisements and campaigns to encourage NGOs and NPOs such as Amnesty International to aid the DPRK with consultants sent from the UN,

ii. considering the DPRK's stance when discussing about giving aid to the DPRK,

4. *Keeping in mind* the need to alleviate previous sanctions that had been enforced by past Security Council resolutions such as 1718/1874/2087/2094 for the purpose of stabilizing the DPRK's economy to ensure its citizen's integrity with having conditions such as but not limited to:

a. alleviating sanctions under the condition that the DPRK follows this resolution,

b. considering harsher conditions to be implemented on

the DPRK if it later changes its stance regarding what had been promised by the DPRK upon this resolution,

c. nations promising to abide by the terms the DPRK makes if it seems fit in further Security Council meetings for the purpose of persuading the DPRK,

d. United Nations Human Rights Organization promoting NGOs and NPOs to inspect conditions in the DPRK after its consent to see the effectiveness of loosening sanctions after being promoted by using methods such but not limited to:

   i. NGOs and NPOs inspecting the conditions before loosening sanctions on the DPRK with the consent of its nations,

   ii. NGOs and NPOs inspecting the conditions in the DPRK after annually loosening sanctions,

   iii. NGOs and NPOs that inspects the conditions of the DPRK's humanitarian status to be reported to the United Nations;

5. *Fully Alarmed* by the fact that the DPRK had been possessing chemical and biological arsenals up to 5,000 tons according to ICG's 2009 report and proclaims the need to do such but not limited to:

   a. The DPRK to sign the Chemical Weapons Convention (CWC)/ Biological and Toxin Weapons Convention (BTWC)/ and the Geneva Convention by 2015 for the purpose of promoting peace and stability in the Korean Peninsula,

b. United Nations Special Commission (UNSCOM) to fully investigate the DPRK's chemical weapons arsenals along with biological and toxin weapons arsenals annually,

c. considering the DPRK's national sovereignty when implementing UNSCOM's inspection with such conditions but not limited to:

    i. having the consent of the DPRK to encourage the DPRK to actively participate in the measures made in this resolution,

    ii. affirming the DPRK's consent annually to remind DPRK of its words;

6. *Recognizes* the need to have multilateral talks between nations like China/ Japan/ USA/ DPRK/ ROK...etc. to promote negotiations between nations by means such as but not limited to:

  a. conducting an immediate six party talk in 2014 for the purpose of promoting peace and stability in the Korean Peninsula,

  b. not having conditions before the conference for having pre-conditions had only halted talks between nations totally;

7. *Remains* to be actively seized upon the matter.

3. Amendments. An amendment is used to either change, strike, or add content to the draft resolution that had been introduced to the floor. When writing an amendment, you should first write which of the three options you want to use and if you

are striking a clause, state which clause to strike (ex. Strike Operative clause 2 sub clause b sub-sub clause iii). If you are willing to change a clause, you should write which clause you will change and write down the correction. And if you are willing to add more content to a clause, you should state which clause you want to add on to and write the clause you have in mind. After you have written your amendment, you should get the approval of the chair before raising your placard to have your amendment approved. While the chair may approve amendments that bring minor changes to a draft-resolution, if there isn't much time left, the chair will only approve an amendment that brings substantive issues to the floor. So to have yours picked among amendments proposed by other delegates, you will need to persuade the chair that what you are trying to amend is something 'big and important.' If the chair recognizes you to come up to the podium, you will need to read what you have proposed and you would have about 90 seconds to persuade others why your amendment should pass. After having 2 speakers for and 2 speakers against the proposed amendment, it would be put into a vote. As you can see, the formal process for amendments is time-consuming and thus it would be better to finish the discussion and amend the draft resolution in the form of a working paper.

4.5. Special Tips & Advice

The special tips are here for you to learn basic skills to improve your performance during sessions. By reading the information below, you will be able to tackle impediments during typical situations with dexterity.

Tip 1. The resolutions in the United Nations are for recommendations only. Only the resolution made in the Security Council has binding power over its member nations. This means that if some delegate in the General Assembly talks about the need to force all nations into doing something, you can tell that delegate that it's not within the GA's power to do so.

The P5 nations

Tip 2. Some conferences in Korea may have unique motions such as the motion to divide the question and the motion to have a P5 meeting (These motions weren't included in the aforementioned chart of points and motions). If a motion to divide the question passes, delegates will have to vote on the resolution clause-by-clause. This motion is useful to utilize when you agree on most clauses in a resolution but disagree with some. If a motion for a P5 meeting passes in the Security Council, P5 nations (USA, France, England, China, and Russia) could temporarily go out of the committee room to discuss something. Another motion that may be present is the motion to change the order of the voting for the resolution. The wording may vary between conferences, but this motion can change the set order for voting on a resolution and may change the result of whether your resolution passes or not. It is an especially useful motion to use when the conference policy makes it so that only one resolution can pass per committee. Generally the three motions mentioned in tip 2 are rarely used in Korean conferences but since there were some conferences like Global Classroom: Seoul and SIGMUN that used some of these motions, I have included them here.

Tip 3. NGOs (Non-Governmental Organizations) are organizations that do the field work. You should never say that NGOs will fund an operation; NGOs are the organizations that are being funded to work on an initiative.

Tip 4. Sometimes you may see a delegate demanding that you become realistic and ask you to tell him/her how the solutions in your resolution will be funded. You may tell him/her that if the committee passes this resolution, this committee's budget will allow the solutions to take action. You may also add that since the committee budget comes from the UN General Budget, if the delegate is so concerned about the difficulty in preparing a feasible amount of finance, the committee may try harder lobbying to bring a larger budget to this committee (wink).

Tip 5. If you seek to form a bloc and lead it, it will be imperative for you to utilize your first unmoderated caucus. The first unmoderated caucus is when most delegates decide which team he/she will be on and thus you should use your time to form a group with other delegates who have similar national stances as you have. First frame the principles in your stances and find others that have similar national visions as you have. I always used note passing to achieve this. Right after the 1st session, when everyone is giving their opening speeches in turn, I used to send note papers to delegates who I wanted to work with to meet during the unmoderated caucus. And by making this sort of reservation, I was able to form a group with relative ease. If however you lose your chance to do so and see others gathering around another delegate, you could still form a group by gathering delegates who are secluded from the already-forming-blocs.

Tip 6. There are certain things you should definitely bring to the conference room if you are participating as a delegate. You should always bring your laptop to write your resolution, several copies of your solution paper/position paper to spread your ideas, and several pens and flash drives. You definitely need your laptop since without it, you won't be able to form a bloc. The owner of a laptop writes down the resolution in the middle of a circle and without it, you will be at a significant disadvantage. Preparing several copies of solution papers and position papers to distribute to other delegates will help your ideas spread through the committee faster. Having several pens and flash drives will allow you to help out other delegates.

Note passing papers

USB drive

Writing utensils

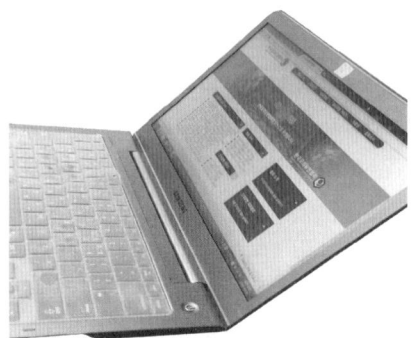
Laptop

Delegate attires

Typical delegate's desk during a conference

Tip 7. After giving your speech after your name is called from the general speakers' list, immediately send a note to the chair saying that you would like to be added to the speaker's list again. By doing so, you will increase your chance of speaking more. Though the content of your speech is vital for you to have influence in your committee, if you don't speak a lot, you won't have the chance to have much influence in the first place.

Tip 8. Though having the ability to speak after preparation is great, you should get used to making impromptu speeches. You will definitely need this ability to rebut other nation's accusations during caucuses. Without the ability to speak after jotting down the main points of what your speech will contain, the chance you'll impress your chairs with your ideas is relatively slim. Because one's ability to perform impromptu

Speak as many times you can © Pete

speeches without rehearsal is gained through lots of practice, you should spend your time before the conference practicing. You don't need to speak fast however, if that's your concern. Your aim should be to make others understand the ideas you present and make others understand the rationale behind them.

Tip 9. If your name is far down the general speaker's list even after you have sent a note to the chair that you'd like to be on the speaker's list, you may want to raise a motion for a moderated or an unmoderated caucus. If your motion passes, you will get a chance you speak again! Usually after 4~5 speakers speak from the general speaker's list, some delegates will raise their placards to make a motion. You should also do that. You shouldn't be afraid to make a motion.

Tip 10. During a conference, you may sometimes see the debate starting to lose its focus or you may want other delegates to focus on a specific topic. If that is the case, you can motion for a moderated caucus and state the reason why you have raised it. If your motion passes, the delegates will only be allowed to discuss the topic you have stated until the moderated caucus ends. If you use the moderated caucus effectively, you will be able to impress the chair by showing your ability to move the debate forward.

Tip 11. Say that you have opened yourself to any and all point of information and a delegate asks you a difficult question that you can't answer. You are stuck and don't know what to say. How should you act? If you are stuck on a question during a point of information, you could simply tell the delegate that you will answer him/her in note form.

Tip 12. If you know your national stance well, you may consider saying "present and voting!" during roll call. If you are the delegate of North Korea (DPRK) and have a firm stance on an issue, you would be able to tell other nations how stubborn you are by saying "present and voting" since this means that you wouldn't be able to abstain during substantive votes. But you should only use this option if you know your national stance well since you wouldn't be able to abstain later if you use this option. Also if the voting records in the UN show that your nation does abstain in the agenda your committee is discussing, saying "present and voting" may not be within your country's best interest; be careful when using it.

Tip 13. Never get on the bad side of a chair. No matter how experienced you are, if you want an award, accept the chair's chairing style. Try your best to remain diplomatic even during breaks since the chair may be watching you; you should be courteous every time. Also, don't raise Point of Order too much. I once raised 5~6 Points of Order in a row thinking that I was showing my knowledge in the Rules of Procedures. But because the Deputy Secretary General saw my chair not being able to answer the questions I had raised and was admonished after the session, I seemed to get on the chair's bad side and ultimately failed to receive an award. If I were wiser, I could have used Points of Inquiry instead of Points of Order. (If you forgot what the two motions are, take a look at the Points and Motions chart in Chapter 1).

Tip 14. Many delegates seem to feel that if they are assigned to a relatively unknown nation like Azerbaijan or a less powerful nation like Zimbabwe, they are at a disadvantage in the award winning process. However this is not true. If you get North Korea in a committee that talks about North Korea's nuclear issues, you *will* be at disadvantage as I once had; however in other cases, you might *even have some advantages*. For instance, by having a lesser known nation, you could have a relatively more flexible national stance. If China states that it supports religious rights, everyone would know that the delegate hadn't done much research on its nation. However if Cote d'Ivoire states that it supports religious rights, not many delegates would have the necessary knowledge to refute that delegate's statement. Also while it may seem that big nations like the P5 lead small nations in a conference, it is only because delegates with rich previous experience are assigned to well-recognized nations. If you do more research than the delegate of USA, you will be the one to lead the debate. As Model UN isn't the actual UN, every delegate truly has an equal voice in a committee. A delegate's skill decides who does what in Model UN.

Tip 15. If you hadn't researched other country's stances but need to form a group with others, you can use some basic indicators to have the best guess whom to work with. Because nations with similar circumstances are close allies, you might want to ask whether it's a nation in the west or in the east. Is it developed, developing, or an underdeveloped nation? Is the country run by a communist party? Is it a democratic nation? Which religion is most prominent in the country? These questions may help you guess which countries you should be allies with. But in the end, you should talk with that delegate to see if your countries' central principles.

Tip 16. Though this is the last tip, it is one of the most important tips. When making your speeches, try to get a single point across the floor. Many delegates try to convey too many ideas to others and, in the process, end up making no point at all. Some delegates even fall in the error of only talking about different statistics. While showing off your research is great and while it is great to see that you have many ideas to speak about, if you try to jam all your knowledge into a 60~90 second speech, you won't get anything across the floor. Try instead to make a single, powerful, idea that resonates throughout your committee. You will be able to find out how other delegates start to adhere to your words and how your ideas are picked up by others in their speeches.

4.6. Award Selections

Every conference has different award criteria. Global Classroom emphasizes a cooperative learning atmosphere and GLIS 6 emphasized how many times one spoke, selecting awardees strictly on tally sheets. Though every conference works according to different standards, most conferences I've seen lately in Korea seemed to pick awardees based on a more holistic manner. For instance, the award criteria below is SIGMUN Winter's award criteria that had been publicly announced to the delegates during its opening ceremony.

Award Criteria Ideals

1. Bring out the true spirit of the committee
   (Follow committee ideals and country stance)
2. Bring out the best of other delegate
   (Ex: Not pre-writing resolution and not enforcing one's opinion over others)
3. Move the debate forward
   (Constructive criticisms and solutions)

Award Criteria

1. Concrete research background
   (Ex: Follow country stance, ROP understanding, etc.)
2. Participation
3. Content/Clarity of speech
4. Manners (to delegates, staffs, and to secretariats)

The award I received in 2013 MUNCCC

5. Tidiness (punctuality to the Code of Conduct)

In a typical three day conference, chairs in respective committees meet with the secretariat in charge of awards at the 2nd night of a conference. In conferences where I've worked, I had every chair give me a list of prospective awardees ranked from 1st to 5th and heard the rationale behind their selections. The list typically doesn't change on the 3rd day but I've seen it change even before the closing ceremony. There sometimes are delegates who try their best until their 2nd day but slack off on the 3rd day. Just remember that awardees may not be finalized until the last minute.

To become an awardee, you need to show the chairs that you are influential. To be influential, you need to make yourself unique by framing your ideas that you can persuade others into following you. Explicit indicators of this phenomenon are the number of times you speak and whether you are the leader of your bloc (main submitter). But just because you aren't a main submitter or just because you speak little doesn't mean that you are automatically eliminated from being a prospective awardee. Some chairs listen closely to the delegate's ideas and if that brings substance to a debate or moves a debate forward, that delegate may be recognized by the chair with an award rather than someone who speaks for the sake of speaking.

Chairs discussing awardees after session

Secretariats discussing awardees

Aspects Chairs Look At When Selecting Awardees

1. How well is the position paper written?
2. How much does the delegate speak throughout the conference?
3. What is the quality of the delegate's speech?
4. Does the delegate abide by his/her national stance?
5. Does the delegate utilize the Rules of Procedures?
6. Does the delegate move the debate forward?
7. Is the delegate leading a group?
8. Are everyone's ideas being included in the group's working papers/resolutions?
9. Does the delegate abide by the logistics of the conference? (Dress codes and punctuality)
10. How well is the resolution written?

Although awards are important, the experience you gain through Model UN should actually be of greater priority. And because you not winning an award don't mean that you have lost your valuable experience, try your best and see what happens. If you simply enjoy the experience and persevere, you will in all likelihood win an award anyway in the future. And since you will only submit the biggest award you receive to your college admissions board (if you are in a high school Model UN circuit), not winning an award here or there won't be much of a problem. This sounds like a cliché but try your best and enjoy the results.

Chapter 5
Post Model UN Activities

I love Model UN. But after doing Model UN for several years, I wanted to explore beyond its horizons in an actual conference or an event in the real world. Thus I have searched for other activities that can be done after one's Model UN career and this chapter is here to share with you some Model UN related activities in Korea. Essentially, the activities mentioned hereafter are activities fit for prospective students who are aiming to major in International Relations or related majors like Political Science.

5.1. Youth Committees

▎ National Human Rights Commission of Korea Textbook Monitoring Youth Committee
(http://www.humanrights.go.kr/00_main/main.jsp)

I've worked as a member of the 5th National Human Rights Commission of Korea Textbook Monitoring Youth Committee and it is an activity I recommend to anyone whose interest lies in human rights. As the name of this activity suggests, one of the main things I did in the committee was looking through textbooks to find aspects that go against human rights. But in order to learn what human rights are, we listened to lectures from a North Korea refugee school principle, LGBT rights activist, etc. Not only that, we worked on a project regarding student human rights on the 'Ordinance of Human Rights for Students'. We

Students in a youth committee discussing with each other

surveyed about 1,500 students on how the ordinance made a few years ago was actually being implemented in the field and presented the result at the National Human Rights Commission of Korea's workshop. A year later, I was also able to find out through a news article that one of the suggestions we made in the textbook was actually implemented. It was extremely satisfying to present the work we had done and see its result impacting the real world.

Poster for an event held by the Human Rights Commission of Korea

- Youth Special Conference
- Youth Participating Committee
- Youth Operating Committee

  (http://www.youth.go.kr/ywith/activity/commission/intro.do#)

The three activities above can be found in the link above. Youth Special Conference is a national youth conference held once a year and Youth Participating Committee is a regional committee discussing youth related policies in each region. Youth Operating Committee is a committee that operates some youth facilities. If you are interested in working with a youth committee under the government, you should definitely check out the link above.

I've only participated in the Youth Participating Committee in 2014 as a member of the Chungcheong-buk do province. Though the activities vary by region, here we wrote policies that dealt with youth activities and made a script for a radio broadcast introducing our committee.

5.2. International Events

- Cross Country Youth Exchange Program
- Korea/China Youth Exchange Program
- International Conferences/Events Program
- Youth Oversees Volunteering Program

▪ Korea/China/Japan Youth Friendship Meeting
(http://iye.youth.go.kr/iye/pgif/odi/view.do)

Activities above are all operated under the Ministry of Gender Equality and Family. Lots of MUNers seemed to participate in at least one of the activities above. Unfortunately, if you participate in one of the activities, you aren't eligible to apply for another activity for 2 years. I haven't participated in one of the activities yet but am aiming to participate in the activities under the International Conferences/ Events Program category. Some activities are very competitive to participate in since some aim to pick national representatives. In most of the activities above, if you are selected, you would be financially aided to some degree. Note that most activities take place abroad and the activities are administered under the Korean government.

5.3. Academics

▪ Coursera (https://www.coursera.org/)

Edx (https://www.edx.org/)

High School- College Related Advanced Studies
(http://up.kcue.or.kr/index.jsp)

Coursera and Edx are two of the most famous massive online education platforms like the Khan Academy. 'High School-College Related Advanced Studies' program, which is a program for high school students to take courses in Korean colleges, is similar to dual enrollment programs in high schools abroad. I've only experienced Coursera and Edx and they were wonderful. There are hundreds of courses online and if you just devote your time, you can learn anything without any financial constraints; the courses are all free if you just audit them. When doing Model UN, there may be times when you feel that your depth of knowledge is too shallow to fully comprehend the topic. Even after preparing for some Advanced Placement exams, you may feel the need to have a stronger academic background and the online platforms are there to satisfy your needs. If you love exploring new topics and learning new things, online education would be a great opportunity to enhance your erudition.

■ International Social Science Conference for Youth
(http://isscy.com/)
■ Korea Social Science Conference for Youth (http://www.kscy.kr/)
■ Creative Critical Thinking (http://journalcct.org/)

ISSCY, KSCY, and CCT are forms of youth thesis contests. I've only linked three out of many different thesis contests in Korea so if you are interested in this particular activity, you can check out the links above.

5.4. Summer Programs

■ Telluride Association Summer Program (TASP)
(http://www.tellurideassociation.org/)
■ UNAOC EF summer school (http://unaocefsummerschool.org/)
■ Hanwha Wingsharers Leadership Conference
(http://www.netcruit.co.kr/html/nanum/sub_01_1.html)

It is extremely difficult to participate in TASP, UNAOC programs. The TASP program is one of the most competitive summer programs to get into and is similar to that of a highly selective college admission. UNAOC-EF summer school is also very competitive with the chance to participate in Korea estimated to be about 1300:1. But since it would be great if you apply and are accepted even through luck, I've linked them here. The TASP program is known to be like an IVY League admission and UNAOC-EF summer school is known to pick applicants who focused on one issue under an organization for many years.

Wingsharers Leadership Conference is also competitive to some extent but has a 10:1 admission rate which is way better than 1300:1. I've participated in the Hanwha Wingsharers Leadership Conference in 2015 and it is something I would really recommend everyone to participate. This leadership conference isn't like any typical leadership conference. Here, Harvard students come as mentors and you are able to learn what they've prepared for almost a year. You may perhaps think of leadership conferences as not being useful and a waste of time. That's what I thought before attending this conference. I actually didn't know what this conference would be like but just applied from curiosity and attended the conference since Hanwha provided full financial aid to all participants. However, while attending the conference, I realized that if I hadn't attended this, I would have lost an experience that could affect my next 1~2 years and beyond. Hanwha Wingsharers Leadership Conference was one of the best experiences I had in my life and I believe that it would be a wonderful experience for you too. I can't put the specific lessons I've learned into words, but I've been inspired by the mentors and through this conference, I was able to acquire a new attitude.

Harvard mentors

5.5. News/Blog Reporter

- Ministry of Justice Reporter Association
  (http://blog.daum.net/mojjustice/8706591)
- Ministry of Environment Reporter Association
  (http://www.me.go.kr/home/web/board/read.do?boardMasterId=39&boardId=358474&menuId=290)
- Ministry of Education, Science and Technology Reporter Association (http://if-blog.tistory.com/)
- Korea Policy Reporter (http://reporter.korea.kr/index.jsp)
- EBS School Reporter Association (http://cafe.naver.com/ebsreporter)

5.6. Debate Competitions

▌ YTN & HUFS Youth English Debating Championship
(http://www.englishdebatingchampionship.co.kr/)

▌ National Schools Debating Championship (http://koreansdc.com/)
▌ Korea University Debate Championship (http://kudc.wordpress.com/)
▌ National Forensics League (http://nsdakorea.org/)
▌ Gwangju Youth English Debating Championship
(http://www.debategfn.or.kr/main_6th.html)

The public speaking skills I've learned through practicing debates were the foundation of my Model UN public speeches. Since you need to speak continuously for about 7 minutes in a debate while the maximum you can speak in Model UN is usually about 1.5 minutes, practicing debate will definitely enable you to speak with dexterity during conference.

5.7. Volunteer Works

- Compassion Mate (http://www.compassion.or.kr/mate/Intro/MateIntro.aspx)
- International Volunteer Organization (http://ivo.or.kr/)
- bbb Korea (http://www.bbbkorea.org/bbbkorea/institution.php)
- Youth Volunteers (http://dovol.youth.go.kr/dovol/index.do#)

The sites above are links to volunteer works that are focused on translation. I've worked as a mate in the Compassion foundation for a year. To elaborate on this activity, Compassion Mates translate beneficiary letters and send them to their benefactors living in Korea and vice versa. It was intriguing for me to read the beneficiary letters at first since I was able to learn how it was like to live without many resources in locations such as Africa. It was educational because I actually got to know how the children I spoke about during Model UN lived their lives. But after translating over 40 hours, I noticed that the contents in the letters overlapped with letters I'd translated previously and slowly lost interest in the activity after a year. But if you're new to this activity, there would be lessons you would gain.

Compassion Mate webpage

Compassion Mate volunteer hours

5.8. Internships

- The Asia Institute (http://www.asia-institute.org/)
- East Asia Institute (http://www.eai.or.kr/korean/index.asp)
- Participation Union (http://www.peoplepower21.org/)

There aren't many internship opportunities that allow the participation of high school students. Internships that do allow high school students' participation requires you to pay a significant fee to get a taste of that experience-usually programs made by companies. Therefore, students seem to rather take advantage of their parent's occupations to earn an internship position. However, there exist some internships that are intended for high school student's participation with the minimal fees. These internships openly recruit students a few times a year and focus on student education. But because information on internship opportunities isn't shared, only students from schools like KIS tend to participate. If you are interested in International Relations, Political Science, or any related fields, you may want to check out the links above. If you are legally an adult, you also become eligible to apply to other internships offered by WFUNA, UNDP Seoul Policy Center, etc.

5.9. Other Websites

■ Youtheca (http://youtheca.com/)

■ MIZY (http://www.mizy.net/)
■ Solmo's House (http://gksthfah96.blog.me/)

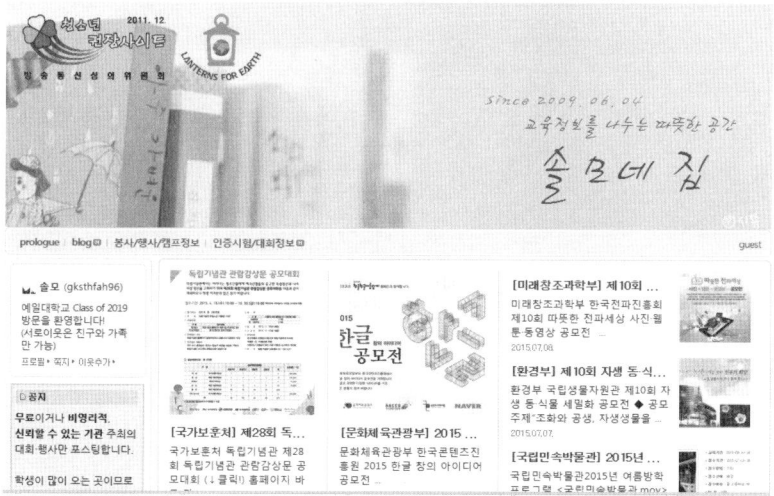

- Allcon (http://www.all-con.co.kr/)
- Spec Up (http://cafe.naver.com/specup)
- Seoul Youth Activities Center (http://www.sy0404.or.kr/)
- Youth Activities Information Service
  (http://www.youth.go.kr/newportal/index.do)

The sites listed above are sites where information on activities is constantly posted. They aren't activities themselves but I linked them above since it would be better for you if you could have your own source to look for yourself. Personally, I received a lot of help from 'Youtheca' and 'Solmo's House'.

Chapter 6
Journey of Model UN

6.1. John Sang-Yup Lee's Experience
Global Vision Christian School, 1997

First Conference: Anxiety to Exuberance

I first got to know Model UN while working as a junior press agent. I saw students my age looking cool in their formal attires discussing serious matters, but I dared not approach a topic that seemed too difficult for me. However, one day when I heard that a high school hosted a middle school conference for rookies (HAFS MIMUN), I felt that it may be a good once-in-a-life-time experience and signed up, feeling ambivalent. On the conference day, I woke up early in the morning feeling anxious. I didn't know anything about Model UN and didn't know how the conference would proceed. All I did was read the provided chair report and search for some news about the topic. The topic, as I still remember it today, was about the Syrian Refugees which I had little or no prior knowledge about.

MIMUN webpage

It was also embarrassing when I got into the conference room because I was the only one who was wearing western business attire; everyone else was in their school uniforms. Though the session started, I didn't know what to do and for the first several hours, remained silent to watch others speak at the podium. The morning's tension lessened after lunch and I slowly raised my placard and was called upon. I made my first speech. Though I don't remember how I spoke during my first speech, I'm sure that it was awful. I remember returning back to my seat with shaking hands. However, that really didn't occur to me at that time. What mattered was that I spoke in front others for the first time. After speaking for the first time, the frequency of raising my placard increased and on the third day, I saw myself instinctively raising my placard to the point where the chair wouldn't call on me so to give others a chance to speak. I didn't win any awards at the conference; however, I was able to absorb the Rules of Procedures and became confident in speaking in front of people.

> "Hearing my throbbing hear beat, I walked toward the podium. Feeling the piercing stares of people in western business attires in front of me, I began forming the words I had jotted down. As time flows, the passion hidden inside my heart flows out like a fire pierced by a dragon. I point out the clashes and solutions to a problem under a beaming spotlight and throw out a dramatic speech toward the audience; Here, I am the protagonist, Here, I can indulge myself into my newfound passion…"

After that exuberating experience of bringing out my passion, I wanted to be good at it. I searched YouTube for videos of speeches and clips from debate competitions. Although I'm not 100% sure whether it helped much, I turned on three hour long debate videos in my bedroom while sleeping in the hopes of unconsciously learning the styles of speech. When my father came home from work, I suggested talking about an issue in English and had mini debates with him to hone my skills. I also attended a debate hakwon-a profit making private education institution common in Korea- for a month to practice debate with others. One day I searched some random keywords in a Korean search engine and accidently found some kind of high school organization for Model UN called KIMC High School Union. I watched some video clips there and received help from some staff members after e-mailing them to inquire about specific rules in the Rules of Procedures. All this effort may have been a tedious task. But as it felt great to be better at something that I had started to love, I was able to push myself.

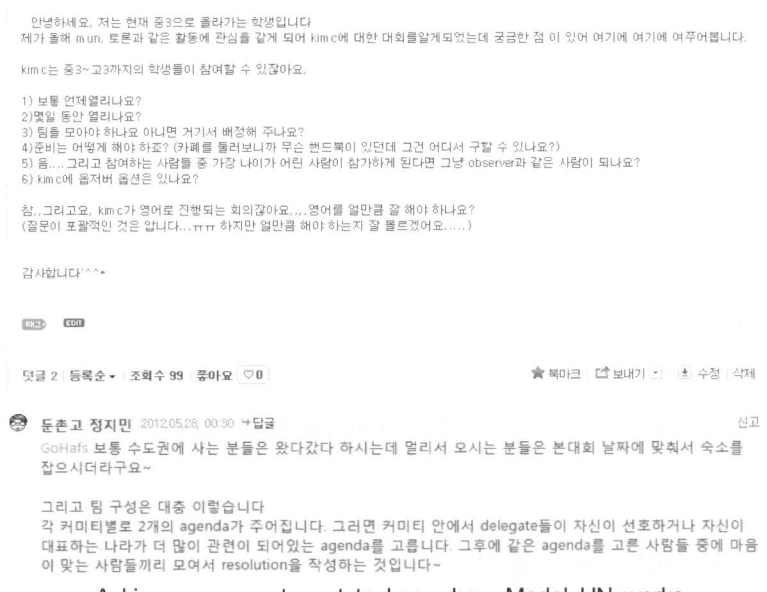

Asking someone to get to know how Model UN works

Starting an Organization

Secretariats discussing to organize a conference

Secretariats discussing to organize a conference

After attending four conferences in 9th grade, I wanted to experience the role of a chair. While randomly typing in Model UN key words into Naver, a Korean search engine, I found a recruiting poster saying that an organization called Global Talent Raising Operation (GTRO) was looking for secretariats. Having some interest, I applied for one of its secretariat positions and was called for its first meeting. Though it may sound absurd, even though I was admitted, I had no plans to actually work as a secretariat at first. I didn't have much experience even as a delegate let alone as a chair to work as a secretariat. Secondly, while my house was is in Seoul, the work place for GTRO was in the rural parts of Korea that were far away from my house. I would have to take a 3~4 hour trip by train to even get to the meeting place and 3~4 hours back. Thirdly, the new found organization, GTRO, had just been started by someone I didn't know so the future of this organization wasn't even clear. But curious to see how it would turn out, after getting permission from my parents, I made the 3 hour ride on the train. I thought that if the other secretariats were fine, I would work with them and if not, just come back home. We had a 3 hour meeting and since I thought that it may end up fine, I decided to participate. The process after that decision wasn't easy though. It wasn't easy to commit 3 hours going and 3 hours returning by train for a 3 hour meeting twice a month while attending a boarding school. I wouldn't have done that if I saw Model UN only as a component to boost my college admission chances.

After organizing the Changwon Advanced Model UN in the rural parts of Korea, Global Talent Raising Operation (GTRO) went through the process of becoming registered as a company and sponsored start-up Model UN conferences both in rural and urban areas of Korea. And as a member of its executive board, I was able to make a sponsorship speech at one of its conferences in 2014. It actually wasn't me who made GTRO the company it has become. GTRO's president worked to do it. But by grabbing the chance to work and by devoting myself to it, I was able to do something I couldn't have done by myself.

GTRO sponsor speech I made in HAIS MUN 1 on Jun. 20 2014

Model UN, Model UN, and Model UN

2013 Best Delegate Camp at UCLA (I am the 8th person from the left)

Public speaking training at UCLA in 2013 Best Delegate Camp

My year in 2013 was filled with Model UN. Starting with four conferences in my 9th grade year, I attended Canada International MUN and several national conferences in Korea during 10th grade. Wanting to experience diverse aspects of Model UN, I also participated as a monitor agent in a college conference and as a camper in a Model UN camp held at UCLA. Through winning awards I was invited to the British Embassy of Korea for a dinner and was enlisted on a newspaper. Winning a premium award at the Korea International Model Congress gave me an opportunity to attend a leadership conference in Australia with a full financial ride including airfare costs. These results were satisfying. But what was really fantastic about Model UN was that I was able to meet people who had similar interests as me. By interacting with people similar to myself, I got to know what other activities people did that are related to Model UN. Through meeting people at Model UN, I began to participate in what others did and thus was able to enlarge my 'comfort zone'. I initially never thought about working in a youth committee under the government but applied and worked as a youth member of the National Human Rights Association of Korea and Chung Cheong Buk-Do province.

In 2014 I attended a Model UN conference called Global Classroom: Seoul. GC: Seoul is one of the conferences that are held in different cities around the world with the Korean conference being hosted by Kyung Hee University. Fortunately,

2014 Leadership conference at Melbourne University

2014 Leadership conference at Melbourne University

I received a Best Delegate award and was admitted to GC's Korea team. In summer of 2014, a total of 10 delegates traveled to New York for the international conference. Our team arrived about 2 days prior to the conference and toured New York while preparing for the conference at night. My teammate and I quickly wrote our position papers while in flight. During the night time preparation time, we pondered upon solutions and perused through the research we had conducted.

Going to New York with other members of the team in 2014

2014 GCIMUN opening ceremony

Exhausted after the 1st day in 2014 GCIMUN

2014 GCIMUN research binder

📖 Spreading Model UN

At the start of 2015 I participated in SIGMUN the WINTER as its Standing Advisor and worked as its Deputy Secretary

General during its summer conference. I worked as a Standing Advisor in a conference called MUNNEO held during the summer of 2015. Also, continuing the work with Global Talent Raising Operation (GTRO) to help establish new found Model UN conferences, I helped make connections between Model UN conferences and the company. Along with these works, I registered the Model UN club I had made in my school as a member of the KIMC High School Union. On the internet, some

Opening speech I made in the 2014 SIGMUN conference

people and I worked to create a platform where people could freely interact on any matters regarding Model UN. I worked as its Vice President since 2013 and helped attract over 1400 members by 2015. The internet café has become Korea's largest on-line Model UN platform. Currently I'm writing this book and wrote a case study of Korea's Model UN to publish in an international research conference.

I am writing this book to talk about Model UN because I had received so much help from others while starting my Model UN career. Because I understand how starting without any relevant background is difficult, I wanted to help others discover relevant information better. Summer of 2015 will likely be the end of my Model UN career that began in 2012. For the past four years Model UN helped me advance both socially and intellectually. I can't imagine what my life would be like without Model UN. I hope that you also attain all the benefits I had attained, if not more, from Model UN.

6.2. Jong Lim's Experience

International Christian School – Uijeongbu, 1997

As I journeyed through high school, I put a lot of emphasis in my life on the impact that certain opportunities can have. An opportunity can be seen as a door opening; leading to all sorts of diverging paths, which then lead to different adventures. To even begin your grand adventure, you have to push yourself through that first door, whatever it may be. You can give yourself that initial push, get on a train bound for success, and find out what you can really do, or you can stay back and watch someone be what you could have been. To the surprise of myself and many others, I opened that first door and it led to another, and another, and another until I realized something very important to my future that can be easily summarized in a Bruce Lee quote-

"To hell with circumstances; I create opportunity." – Bruce Lee, Martial Artist

My first door was Model UN or MUN. This is the door that started it all. However, for a while, that door was hard to get open. Was it locked? Was someone blocking it from the other side? Those are usually reasonable questions to ask when you have trouble opening a door. My problem was simpler than that though. Just like how I didn't know how to properly open soda cans until I was thirteen, I didn't know how to open this first door until my third conference. Knowing this, it's easy to imagine how my first conference went. Silence. That was my contribution on the first day. I didn't raise my placard and nor did I talk to anyone during the unmoderated caucuses. Meeting new people wasn't something I was cool with yet and neither was being near people I haven't met yet. I was an introverted and antisocial boiling soup. *Clearly a good combination for MUN.* The second day was slightly more active. I started talking with other delegates during caucuses (small talk and not about the Gaza strip, but it was a start) and received a note from the chair encouraging me to speak. During an unmoderated caucus, one of the delegates mentioned that she noticed the delegate of the U.S.A. and the delegate of Iran working together. Since they weren't really representing their countries (also because she was bored), she suggested making a point of order and asking the delegates to walk out of the room due to their behavior. It seemed like fun, so I participated in the epic walkout which our chair complimented us for because of the fact that this happens in the actual United Nations every now and then. Promptly after this, everyone who walked out had to go to the podium and give a short apology to the delegates who had not walked out. Apparently they felt it was unprofessional and rude. That was my entire YMUN Korea experience: small talk, a walkout, and an apology. When it was finally over, I contemplated whether it was worth the money and time. I felt defeated because I didn't do much and didn't feel like I learned much. I felt lost and unsure of how I would do if I ever tried this again. With some encouragement from my school's MUN president and adviser, I marched on. This was my beginning and it felt like a very disappointing beginning.

A few days later, our school hosted its first mandatory high school-wide MUN conference, ICSMUN. Every high school student was required to participate (grades being the incentive) and of course, people would have higher expectations of me since I was one of the few people who knew what the United Nations was, and I was actually in the club. The experience from my first conference helped me know what to do and how to research. Although I had not participated, observing other delegates had helped me learn. I main-submitted and wrote a resolution, mostly on my own because most people had no idea what they were doing. I spoke a few times and fashioned myself with several points of information. The conference went smoothly and I got more used to the environment and atmosphere of MUN. However, it became clear that the reason this event seemed significantly easier was because I was with people I already knew. In the next school semester, I attended my third conference, as the delegate of Peru in the Environmental Commission. This conference was maybe twice or so as big as my first one. With more people, came more intimidation. This conference was conducted using the THIMUN format, so this time I was required to give an opening speech. I researched my topics thoroughly, determined to do better and speak more. As the session began, I encountered an issue. The opening speech that I wrote before was saved on my computer and I wasn't allowed to bring it to the podium during my opening speech. Peru starts with P, so luckily I wasn't first. I hastily wrote down an opening speech just before they got to my delegation. I still struggled with basic MUN skills such as speaking in front of people and terminology. During the debate, I spoke a bit, but my voice wasn't exactly filled with confidence. I was still stammering and pausing. I often couldn't think of what to say and the chair once asked if I would like to answer in note form after a POI. My chair encouraged me to try to speak during a break. She was friendly and spoke as though she was a friend and not a chair. Everyone in this conference was friendly and social, not just our chair, which made me open up a lot more and talk to a lot more people than I usually do. It was a steady process, but I became more social during breaks, more articulate, and better at debate. Now that I look back, it was a transformation that I would describe using words like exponential, progressive, or simply awesome. After this transformation, I had a much clearer idea in my head of what I was supposed to be doing and how to do it. What began inside of me was not just a learning experience after that conference, but a thirst- a hunger. A thirst to learn more about MUN and to improve my skills. A hunger to learn more about the world and how to make a difference. I was at that point, and still am, of being a single cog in something greater, and I wanted to turn and never stop moving forward. The door was open, I walked out, and I started running.

In my junior year, I added newspaper club and National Honor Society to my list of extracurricular activities I was a part of. I became much more proactive and passionate about MUN. For my fourth conference, I swept through it with confidence and drafted a resolution. I no longer stuttered and I was able to think of speeches on the spot without writing them beforehand.

Researching became as easy as breathing and people started to ask me for advice related to MUN. At school, I became known as a MUN fanatic, a title that I held with pride. One of the paths that opened up was a leadership conference, where I learned what leadership truly meant and how to influence others. This prepared me for my first experience as a student officer of a MUN conference. The school-wide conference had swung around again, but this time I was a forum president. The responsibility felt overwhelming at first and there were many times when my assistant president gave me a little whisper to correct a mistake I made. I knew the Rules of Procedure like the back of my hand and I made sure that my delegates felt the same way. There was a personal connection with many of the delegates who struggled to speak or for whom it was their first conference. I tried my best to help them as I knew exactly how they felt just a year prior. I told them that by speaking even once, they were already better than I was at my first conference. Between that experience and my next conference, I purposely tried putting myself in situations where I would have to interact with new people such as at film festivals or forums. Finally, the time for my sixth conference had come. This was when I felt my skills were at my prime and the conference was the same as my first one, YMUN Korea. I had returned, a year later and a year stronger and a year smarter. Abbreviations such as OECD, IAEA, and LEDC were no longer a foreign language to me, but now they were my language; a pool of jargon that I felt comfortable swimming in.

It was time to see how much I'd progressed in a year. I was now fully equipped with a massive research binder that I marveled at during my first YMUN Korea, filled with copious amounts of notes and research. The conference started and we sped through the opening speeches. The format of the conference was a hybrid between UNA-USA and THIMUN, adding a bit of a challenge, but not too much. I arduously worked together with other delegates and helped newer delegates learn the process as a whole. I felt a thrill, a rushing sensation that felt so intense that my blood was like an avalanche, fervently debating. The atmosphere was strong and the committee developed several ways of having fair elections in countries and mitigating social issues in homogenous countries. This conference was truly the best I ever had as a delegate in terms of performance and it was truly where I was able to debate at the best of my ability. When I compare my first YMUN Korea with the second, I see a tremendous amount of improvement. More importantly, I see how much not giving up benefitted me in the long run. Opening that door and taking that first step is what got me to this point. With the end of my junior year of high school came another major door opening in my life: my appointment as MUN president of my school.

The beginning of my new time as president was evidently tough. I received little mentoring from my predecessor, but I was determined to try to lead the club into battle. Almost all of the members were completely new and much younger than last year's members. It was difficult learning to get their attention when they weren't listening and even more difficult to get people to do the work required for conferences. To be honest, being in that position was a thousand times more stressful than being a delegate. To put it bluntly, it was a struggle. The first semester of my senior year felt like a learning experience as a president and as a leader. In most of my conferences in my senior year except for one, I served as a student officer. The level of experience that I had obviously made me qualified for the position, but what I had to learn in that first semester was how to communicate on a level that was understandable and friendly. My vice president helped, of course, but I was the face and symbol that was held responsible for any discrepancies. The greatest test of my leadership capabilities that year, however, was not my term as MUN president, but as Secretary General. During the summer before the school year started, the director of my school nonchalantly suggested hosting a MUN conference. Without a doubt, organizing and starting a new MUN conference would be a daunting task for a small school without proper funding. My passion for MUN hadn't gone dry. Just that mere suggestion was enough to get me started on thinking of how to get this project started. I quickly started brainstorming and discussing ideas with my vice-president, and we decided to partner with another small school. It was determined that I would be the Secretary General and the MUN president of the other school would be the Deputy Secretary General. I quickly organized a small secretariat of five members and dedicated the biggest portion of my time and energy to the conference, which would be called MUNexus. I juggled being the president of my school's MUN with being the Secretary General of MUNexus with multiple chair positions, but the one I looked at the most was MUNexus. The director of my school referred to it as my brain child. I thought of it as my magnum opus. We recruited chairs for the conference and four schools were in attendance, two of which were completely new to MUN. Although there were a few hiccups, there was extremely positive feedback from teachers, delegates, and officers. To sum it up, it was truly one of the proudest moments of my life. But in my final speech to the delegates of MUNexus, I reminded everyone that this was simply the first step of a long journey. I told them that if they spoke even once, they had already done better than I had at my first conference, by taking that first step.

To me and many other people, MUN is more than just something to stick onto a college application. Although I must say that MUN probably helped me a considerable amount into getting accepted to college, I believe it is the skills and confidence that MUN has given me that has truly helped me grow as a person and in turn, lead to my college acceptances. Many doors had been opened during MUNexus and it filled me with joy to think that I had sent many delegates off on a journey with a final message in my closing ceremony speech. A message that I also would like to send off to those reading this right now is a quote from physicist Stephen Hawking, "However bad life may seem, there is always something you can do, and succeed at. While there's life, there is hope." So approach the world and heal its wounds.

6.3. Rinchong Kim's Experience
Whimoon High School, 1997

I'm not someone with a flamboyant Model UN career, but I can tell you with confidence that I've got a passion for it. As of February 2015, I've participated in 13 Model UN conferences: seven times as a delegate, once as a chair, and five times as a secretariat and have also worked as the vice president of a high school Model UN Union which consists of 30 member school. Through these experiences, I've learned many valuable lessons.

I started Model UN in GLIS MUN 7. Like most first MUNers, I didn't understand the Rules of Procedures at first, used lots of 1st person pronouns, and didn't know how to write resolutions. However, I found myself getting used to these aspects of Model UN as I gained more experience.

To get used to Model UN, I went up to the podium and made numerous speeches. And though the speeches themselves weren't the best, I attained confidence through its practice. Rookie delegates tend to just sit down and make no speeches at all throughout the sessions-saying that they aren't familiar with the

Model UN atmosphere. But I just sitting on your seat won't help you to become familiar with Model UN. You should fully indulge yourself in it. Instead of doing nothing, it would better to ask other delegates or chairs about the overall process of Model UN. You should ask someone to help you if it's hard to do it alone.

After GLIS MUN 7, I attended three more conferences during the winter as a delegate. At those conferences, I met people who made huge impacts in my life. Since then meeting new people has become one of the reasons why I participate in Model UN. It is great to know someone in Model UN because you and the other person are likely to have similar goals and dreams. You can help each other out.

I never thought I would be managing a union with over 25 member schools but eventually became the KIMC union's vice president after winter. As the vice president of the KIMC High School Union, I worked to organize numerous unofficial sessions. During the process I learned how to manage budgets and how to use designing tools. I asked my teachers if I could borrow classrooms for some session and prepared for a Model UN conference. We were able to aggregate 170 delegates and had to stop the registration before its deadline. While working on many projects, I believe I was able to learn what responsibility is and how to lead others as a secretariat.

My first experience as a secretariat pushed me to another level: making my own Model UN conference. We came up with the name HAIS MUN and started organizing it from scratch. As this was a new conference, it was hard to get sponsors to create one. But we were able to attain knowledge and skills through facing various difficulties. As the Deputy Secretary General of HAIS MUN, I went over the work done by other secretariats and created its website. Though we had some conflicts on who does what during the process, we persevered to continue. And by persevering, we learned to cooperate and finally made a wonderful conference.

I believe that Model UN is an educational platform that is useful for people to interact with others who have similar interests and also a platform to hone one's skills. Because Model UN operates for the educational values of all participants, it is worthwhile to participate even when you don't receive awards; you would see yourself become enhanced after each conference. Attend a Model UN conference and improve your skills.

6.4. Danny Hong's Experience
Kyung Hee University, 1996

Model United Nations (MUN) has changed my life. Having lived in the United States for over ten years and suddenly returned to Korea right before my freshman year, I had a hard time adjusting to my new life. I did not know the Korean language, and as a result, I lost all confidence, as I could not properly express my opinions due to the fact that I had only learned the Korean Alphabet right after I had returned. I also had no understanding of the culture as I had never truly lived in a country established on Confucianism ideals. Most importantly, I had nearly no friends, as all of the ones I had were back in America, and it was rather difficult to make new friends when you can't communicate with them. However, this all changed when I entered MUNOS (Model United Nations Of Seoul) in my freshman year.

At first, I was forced by my parents to participate and was extremely overwhelmed when I first arrived at the COEX mall exhibition hall to participate in the conference. MUNOS, being one of the biggest MUN conferences in Korea, had well over a thousand participants. In addition to that, everyone was wearing a suit as well as speaking English to one another, something that I had not seen before in my life. This made me nervous, especially when I sat down at my conference table not knowing anyone. However, soon I realized that I had worried in vain. Everyone was extremely kind, and many of them tried to help me understand the Rules Of Procedure (ROP) as this was my first Model UN. Furthermore, it was relatively easy to relate with them because almost all of them had experience overseas in an English-speaking environments. This made it significantly easier for me to approach them and ask for help or advice. Due to this, although I was beyond nervous and scared at first, I was able to prepare and give my first speech in a Model UN conference with confidence. After I gave my speech, my mind was instantly relieved, as doing so was not as difficult as I had imagined. Consequently, I kept on preparing and giving speeches, and with every new speech, I could feel the impact and importance of my words improving. The conference lasted for around three days and during those three days I had talked more than I ever had since returning to Korea. Although I was unable to receive a prize, I gained something much more valuable than that: confidence.

Soon after, I asked my parents if I could attend MUNCCC (Model United Nations Climate Change Conference), to which they complied. In this conference, there were a collection of experienced debaters and Model UN veterans, particularly in my committee of Climate Finance. Due to the heavy atmosphere provided by these members, I was rather shy at first and was afraid to present my thoughts. However, after the first conference, I began to realize that there was truly nothing to be afraid of, and made up my mind to begin giving speeches. After doing so, the confidence I had found at MUNOS was re-attained, and I continued to express my opinions. Yet something was different from my experience at MUNOS. After the first day, some of the members of our committee went to eat dinner together and it was then that many of the members of our group took interest in me because of the huge cultural difference that I had with them. This was mainly in part due to the fact that I did not know I had to use honorifics with individuals that were only a year older than me. Although these individuals were rather shocked at first, they understood me because of their past experiences, and began to teach me about Korean culture. This allowed me to become extremely close with some of them, even to the point in which I can say that my current two closest friends are people that I met at this conference. Once again, although I did not receive a prize in MUNCCC, cultural experiences that me and my friends experienced during this time was worth much more than that to me.

The next conference that I attended was KMUN (Korea Model United Nations). Learning from my mistakes from the past conference as well as learning from the veteran colleagues that I had met at MUNCCC, I began to start lobbying for the first time in my Model UN career. The extent to which I lobbied was to the point where our resolution group had over forty-three members out of a total fifty member states, even before the conference had started. It was at this conference that I was the true main submitter of the resolution for the first time and because of our abundance of supporters, our resolutions were passed with a consensus vote.

However to my dismay, I did not receive a prize at this conference despite the large contribution that I believe I had made to it, as I became rather aggressive and arrogant in my speeches. Although the results were disappointing at first, thinking back, I believe I still learned much from this conference, as I had learned about the importance of both humility and leadership. This allowed me to become class president four times over the course of the next two years.

Following the results of KMUN, I began to question whether I should continue participating in Model UNs as I had not been able to receive a prize despite the great amount of time and effort I put into preparing for them. However, after receiving much support from both my newly made friends as well as my family, I participated in YMUN (Yale Model United Nations) and was able to receive the outstanding delegate award by applying the skills and lessons I had learned through my previous Model UNs. This was a huge boost to my confidence. However this did not last long due to my second participation in MUNCCC. Once again in this conference, the members of my committee were like the elite and very experienced. But regardless of the intense atmosphere of our committee, I was able to overcome the fear that I had experienced in my first MUNCCC and was the main submitter of both the approved resolutions. Yet this time, because of the difficulty I had writing a resolution during and after the conference due to time constraints, I wrote a resolution ahead of time, which was against the conference regulations. Due to this, I was excluded from the award consideration, which instigated me to continue my questioning of whether Model UNs were a good fit for me or not. This doubt led me to cease my participation in Model UNs for a year.

However, with the various lessons and skills I learned from my previous Model UNs, I become accepted to Kyung Hee University's College of International Studies. This sparked my interest in Model UNs once more, as Kyung Hee University is famous for its Model UN Secretariat. This led me to participate in Global Classrooms: Seoul (GC), which was sponsored by my new school. However, this conference was different from anything that I had ever experienced. Until now, I had only done high school Model UNs, but to challenge myself as well as meet my alumni, I chose to enter the University Division of GC. In this conference, I was appointed with the Agenda of assessing the MDGs (Millennium Development Goals) and establishing new STGs (Sustainable Development Goals). This was extremely difficult for me as there was too much to prepare since the agenda itself was over ten times bigger than an average high school Model UN agenda. However, through this, I began to understand that Model UNs are not simply about lobbying, giving speeches, and writing resolutions, but also require members to look beyond that to the bigger picture, and identifying the factors that prevent the actual United Nations from addressing such problems. Consequent to this enlightenment, as well as with much sheer luck, I was able to receive the Honorable Mentions Award in the University Committee, even before becoming a University student. This gave me the confidence and desire needed in order to continue my path through Model UNs, to become a chair and eventually a secretariat.

 I first entered the Model UN society thinking that it was a way to improve my chance in the college admissions process. Although this is somewhat true, I began to realize now that

Model UN is much more than that. It is a way of life, and can change your way of life. It certainly did for me, as it gave me the confidence, cultural understanding, support, leadership, humility, desire, as well as countless more lessons that were needed in order for me to become the person I am today. Perhaps participation can do that much, and maybe even more, for you as well.

6.5. MaryAnn Shim's Experience

Lancaster Catholic High School, 1997

Model UN was the biggest watershed of my life. But before talking my experiences, I want to let you know my past: I was not a *standard student*. When I was in 6th grade, I was elected as the president of student council; After the election, all the members of parents' association of my school dissented that. "I cannot accept her as a president, who should be a paragon of all the students!" they argued. Apparently, I wasn't a paragon of others. One week after the start of middle school, in 7th grade, the teacher's office was like my homeroom. Also while the curfew which was set by my parents was 9 p.m., the curfew which I held onto myself was 1 AM. Thus my parents sent me to the United States hoping for some sort of development. However I ruined their wish in the US. The nation of freedom without my parents who tried to control me was a perfect condition for me to roam freely without any constraints.

But everything changed during the rise of a sophomore year. I applied for a Model UN event in Korea because I would get a volunteering certification for my school's requirement of a diploma. I did not expect much about contents of the conference because it was out of my interest. I did not want to give an attention to that since I felt the name of the conference, *Model UN*, too boring. But it had changed my life. While I thought I would obviously be "better" than others since I attended a school in the States, during three days of conference, I could not understand almost half of the participants' conversations and debates since they used high quality vocabularies and sentence structures that I had never used and learned before. Participating delegates discussed global issues that I had never heard about. Furthermore, the thing that shocked me the most was that they were all my peers. My thought after the conference was: "What did I do last 16 years?" Model UN came as a huge shock to me.

I went back to the United States after my turning point and started to study to be able to compete with delegates in that Model UN. I got straight As, which was the highest GPA in my class. Teachers, my friends, and even my parents and family said that it was a miracle because my past GPA was like straight Cs. Moreover, I participated in several Model UN conferences in the United States and won some awards, too. Lastly for the first time in my life, I searched universities, majors and jobs to set my goals since I realized that all the delegates of Model UN who I have met had their own goals. Currently I want to major international politics in the university and work in global organizations such as UN. My life was influenced by Model UN. By interacting with accomplished peers in Model UN, the fundamentals of my life had shifted.

I cannot describe in words what Model UN means to me. However it is clear that through Model UN I have learned and experienced amazing things that transformed my life. By doing Model UN, I was able to set my goal and drive myself to my future with passion. I believe that Model UN would also lead your life to success.

6.6. Gayoon Lee's Experience
Sogang University, 1996

Suddenly it has become common for me to ask people "Is that another Model UN? From where?" As a person who has gone through the transitional period of Model UN, from the very beginning all the way to the very prosperous present of it, I was and am a bit shocked that there are so many of them today. The news that this book will be published soon also reminds me of the strengthened position of Model UN nowadays. Amazingly, despite the great numbers, almost every Model UN succeeds to fill their delegation caps. And here my doubt arose. Why are all the students eager to participate in this event? Clearly one major reason for this is to build so-called "specs", which are fancy-looking extracurricular activities that help make their possessors shine and stand out from amongst the tons of other college applicants. Here I will tell you how Model UN helped me enter my university and how it can help you to also get into the school you want.

My Model United Nation experiences were included in all of the 10 college essays I wrote. I wrote about my experiences it in the essays for the International Studies and Relationships departments of course, but also for the Art department which is not related to Model UN. Luckily I got accepted to the Art and Technology major in a Korean university with that essay. And I believe it suggests some meanings that admissions officers consider that Model UN is influential not only for being an academically reinforcing agent, but also as a factor that helps students grow internally. Most college admission officers are looking for your potentials, humanities, and what you have felt and how you matured from the life events you have gone through. For someone normal like me who am stuck with the typical high school routine, Model UN acted as a stimulant that helped me break away from my daily schedule. The same everyday life rigidifies your thinking but Model UN inspires you in various ways. Your college essays will unconsciously become lavished with the fresh paradigm of your life events and mature perspectives from the experiences you will attain from Model UN.

By talking about international issues such as sanitation problems, funding, human rights issues, and civil wars in African countries in Model UN conferences, I was able to understand the international society and the national stances of different nations. Furthermore, this knowledge enabled me to make better response to the questions I was asked in the college interview process. This is because no matter what the major is, showing admissions officers that you are an enlightened citizen in the global society is vital. For example if you dream of becoming an international journalist, you can bring up the story about a Syrian girl who wanted to become a physicist but could not get a proper education due to the situation of her government in substantiating her dream. Also by having background knowledge prior to the interview, you can provide richer responses than other applicants on issues regarding Model UN topics that include human rights, political unrest, and etc.

Model UN is also helpful in the college entrance process in that it shows how you have developed yourself. My position while doing Model UN changed from being a participating delegate to one getting prizes, to being chairs, and then a secretariat and that process developed my image as a hard working person who likes to develop their leadership to the admissions officers. Moreover, because Model UN is not only an academic event but also one that is very social, it will help you attain human networks for your college admissions process and beyond. One of the most cherishing aspects I received from my

Model UN career is the social network and friends I made there. By participating in numerous Model UN conferences, I met various kinds of people from different countries who shared diverse interests. This means that you will easily get chances to meet more people and widen your social relationships which can help you in many ways. Some of the students I've met during conferences were already students of the schools that I was dreaming of attending so I could get a proofreading assistance from them before I submitted my essays to college. Some of them were applying to the same college and the same major as me, and so we met up to create a study group or to simply help each other relieve stress. And because some of them were working in real jobs, I was able to get an internship in a firm, get another position for a larger contest, or get a chance to be published in a magazine, etc. Be professional and diplomatic during the session, but be social when it is time. Then you will realize how Model UN can establish a foothold to help you move toward the wider society, which will make you become more of a qualified person for your dream colleges. Chances do not walk to you automatically. You should try hard and actively pursue your dreams.

College officers want you to see who you are and then will decide whether the 'real you' the college officials find deserves to be their student. So in the first place, think about yourself. Does the 'real you' deserve to get the entrance card for that college? If the answer from the deepest part of you is "not yet", try to make yourself qualified enough. I found my answer to be "no" when I was a freshman in high school. But after going through all the Model UN conferences, I finally was able to think I could be the right person for my dream university. This sense of reasonable confidence will lead you to the best results. The point is that Model UN is an activity that develops you. Although attending a few Model UN conferences without having any affections for them will not develop or enhance your standing, if you indulge yourself in it and truly try to develop yourself, you would one day find yourself on the campus of your dream school.

6.7. Min Seok Park's Experience
Korea University, 1996

Many people believe that Model UN will make it advantageous for them to enter a university. However, it is rather the opposite. Doing Model UN a lot may not appeal to professors to pick you as their student. But I believe that Model UN helps you to enter the university you want to in an indirect manner.

It was very hard for me to participate in various Model UNs held in Seoul since I lived in Busan. I had to spend 6 hours on a train whenever there were chair/secretariat meetings. Many people believed this would make it hard for me to focus on my studies because time is limited to 24 hours a day and I had to spend a lot of time doing Model UN. However Model UN acted as a motivator and a refresher for my life. I was able to find my dream while doing Model UN and this charged me to keep on my efforts with my academics. Doing Model UN on the weekends allowed me to focus on studying intensely during weekdays at my school. And consequently Model UN helped me attain a great motivation that led to a great GPA.

Model UN may not act as a direct key to success in terms of university admissions. But it will indirectly lead you to a university by letting you find your dream and motivating yourself so that you can be better with your studies.

Model UN and College Admissions

Speaking of college admissions, you may want to check out the 29 page booklet made by Best Delegate Institute named "How Model UN Can Help You Get into College: Advice, Stories, and Inspiration By Model UN Students".

(http://bestdelegate.com/wp-content/uploads/2010/11/How-Model-UN-Can-Help-You-Get-Into-College-Final-2010-11-15.pdf)

Chapter 7
Additional Resources

7.1. List of Model UN Events in Korea

Name/Info	Website	Region	Schedule
1. CSIAMUN	www.csia2014.wordpress.com	Gapeong	February
2. GC: Seoul	www.kicmun.org	Suwon	January
3. KMUN (Ehwa)	www.kmun.or.kr	Seoul	May
4. MUNCCC	mcop.ytn.co.kr	Seoul	July
5. KHSMUN	www.khsmun.org	Seoul	August
6. MUNOS	edu.chosun.com/leadkorea	Seoul	July
7. NMUN Korea	www.unarok.org	(Changes)	July
8. Yonsei MUN	ymun.org	Seoul	January
9. AKYD MUN	akyd.kr.pe	Daegu	December
10. CAMUN	café.naver.com/camun7.cafe	Changwon	August
11. GLIS MUN	glis.co.kr	Seoul	January / August
12. GYMUN	club.cyworld.com/bitgoeulMUN	Gwangju	August
13. HAIS MUN	www.haismun.org	Seoul	January / August
14. IMUN	café.naver.com/imun2013	Incheon	December

Name/Info	Website	Region	Schedule
15. JOINED MUN	joinedmuninfo.wix.com/joined-secretariat	Jeju Island	September
16. KAYMUN	www.kaymun.co.kr	(Changes)	(Changes)
17. KMUN (Korea)	www.kmun.net	Seoul	January
18. KYMUN	www.kymun.org	Jeju Island	June
19. MIMUN	café.naver.com/hafsmimun2013	Gyeonggi-do	August
20. MUNIEVU	café.naver.com/munievu1	Daejeon	February
21. SEOMUN	seomunkorea.com	Seoul	November
22. SNUMUN	www.snumun.org	Seoul	January
23. Seoul Summit	www.seoulsummit.org	Seoul	August
24. SKYMUN	www.skymun.com	Daegu	February
25. SIGMUN	www.sigmun.oa.to	Seoul	January / July
26. Yale MUN: Korea	ymunkorea.yira.org	Seoul	May
27. YOUMUN	www.haeyum.org	Gwangju	July
28. Handong Global Leadership Academy	camp.handong.edu	Pohang	July
29. KIMUN Workshop	www.kicmun.org	Suwon	July
30. WFUNA Youth Camp: Korea	www.wfuna.or.kr	Suwon	January / July

※ Time of Research: Summer of 2014

The thirty Model UN events above are organized by different secretariats every year and thus detailed information such as conference schedule may vary from year to year. Some conferences may not even exist by the time you read this book. You should check out each conference through its website to get the most updated information.

7.2. Glossary of Model UN Terminologies

Abstain	A delegate may abstain during a substantive voting procedure. This means that the delegates don't vote either for or against the matter being vote on.
Adjourn	A motion may be raised to adjourn the session/meeting and the session/meeting would stop temporarily.
Agenda	The topic which the committee has to talk about.
Amendment	A change proposed in the draft resolution. (Most Korean conferences don't have friendly amendments).
Background guide	Same term used for chair reports written by the chairs to help delegates get started with their research.
Binding	Having legal force over UN member states. (ex. Resolution of the Security Council).
Bloc	A group of nations (delegates) who work for their resolution.
Caucus	A term including both moderated and unmoderated caucuses. It is another style of discussing that is different from the general debate.
Chairs	Another term for student officers. Chairs moderate committees.
DAIS	Another term for student officers. DAIS moderate committees.
Decorum	Order. The chairs usually tell their delegates to mind their decorum if the committee is too noisy.
Delegate	One of the representatives of a given country.
Delegation	A group of representatives (delegates) of a given country. Most conferences in Korea only have 1 delegate assigned per nation. 'Double Delegate' is a form of a delegation.
Division of the Question	A kind of motion to separately vote on clauses in a draft-resolution. This motion is almost never used in Korean conferences although its concept exists in Security Councils.
Draft Resolution	A resolution formatted paper that hasn't been passed through the committee's voting but has been approved by the chair.

Faculty Advisor	Usually a teacher in charge of a delegation. This concept isn't used in most Korean conferences. (There are no faculty advisors except for in schools like international schools and some foreign language schools).
Flow of Debate	The movement of how the conference proceeds.
Gavel	A small hammer like object. Though gavels are given to awardees in international conferences, most Korean conferences do not have these (Thus terms such as 'gavel hunting' doesn't exist).
Formal Debate	Default mode of debate where you have the speakers' list and the delegates go to the podium to give a speech.
Head Delegate	The leader of a model club/delegation/school. Most Korean conferences do not have this concept as most conferences operate through a single-delegation system. Although international schools seem to have these concepts as they attend a conference in groups.
Member State	Country that ratified the Charter of the United Nations and is a formal member of UN's General Assembly.
Merging	Combining two different draft resolutions or working papers.
Moderated Caucus	Form of debate where a delegate can make a speech next to his/her seat after being picked by the chair on the spot. This from of debate saves time and facilitates debate from not needing to wait for one's turn on the often long Speakers' List.
Motion	Request made by the delegate aimed to facilitate the flow of the conference in a certain way.
Observer	In Korea's Model UN, observers are students who've registered as an observer to attend the conference-usually to learn how Model UN works before actually attending a conference as a delegate.
On the floor	If something is "on the floor" it means that the document has been recognized by the chair and now can officially be discussed.
Operative Clause	The part in a resolution that proposes the solutions of the agenda.
Page	Another term for administrative staff. This term doesn't exist in Korean Model UN conferences.
Placard	A sign that has a country name. Delegates raise it if they are willing to be recognized by the chair.

Point	A request made by a delegate. Like motions, there are different kinds of points; all of which serve different functions.
Position Paper	A summary of a country's position on the agenda that needs to be sent to the chair before a (UNA-USA formatted) conference.
Pre-ambulatory Clauses	Clauses in the resolution (or in the draft resolution) that describe the problems of an issue and serves as a general atmosphere of the resolution. Unlike operative clauses, pre-ambulatory clauses usually can't be modified.
Procedural Matters	Process of how a committee is run (unlike substantive matters which deals with the agenda being debated). During procedural votes, delegates may not abstain.
Quorum	The minimum number of delegates needed to be present in order to begin a committee.
Rapporteur	A term similar to that of a vice-chair. Korean conferences do not use this term, however.
Resolution	An agreed document between the member states of the United Nation that consists of solutions to its agenda. While resolutions are simply recommendations, resolutions made in the Security Council have binding power.
Right of Reply	The right to address an insulting remark made by another delegate. It can only be raised when one is personally offended and only after a request sent to the chair for the right of reply has been approved.
Roll Call	Similar to roll calls done in school. When the chair calls out a country, delegates may either answer "present" or "present and voting". Delegate who has answered "present and voting" may not abstain on substantive votes.
Rules of Procedure	The rules that governs Model UN conference.
Second	An acknowledgement of a delegate meaning that he/she approves the motion raised by another delegate. Seconds are usually used in THIMUN styled Model UNs.
Signatory	Countries that are willing to see the amendment/draft resolution discussed on the floor (A signatory does not necessarily mean that a nation supports the amendment/ draft resolution).
Simple Majority	More than half.

Speakers' List	A list of countries selected to speak during a general debate. Usually you can send notes to the chair to be added again on the speakers' list.
Sponsor	One of the writers of a draft resolution.
Substantive Matter	Matters having to do with the topic being discussed. Substantive voting includes votes on draft resolutions or amendments and abstentions are allowed if a delegate hasn't answered "present and voting" during the most recent roll call.
Unmoderated Caucus	A type of caucus where delegates can freely roam around the room to discuss anything about the agenda without any formalized structures. Draft resolutions are usually written during this period.
Working Paper	It is an unofficial document with delegates' ideas. While working papers don't have formats, they frequently take the form of a draft-resolution.
Veto Power	A power the P5 nations (USA, France, England, China, and Russia) have in the Security Council. When one of the P5 nations votes against a draft resolution in the Security Council, it acts as a veto and the voted clause automatically fails.
Vote	Expressing one's opinion as supporting, abstaining, or going against the proposed issue.
Voting Procedure	A period when delegates vote. Staff locks the door during this period and members outside the committee room (for some reason such as a bathroom break) can't vote.
Yield	A delegate's option if he/she has some time left after his/her speech. There are typically three different yields: yielding to the chair, to questions, or to another delegate. If a delegate yields to the chair, he/she should then just go back to his/her seat. If a delegate yields to questions, he/she should state how many questions he/she is willing to accept and answer the questions proposed by other delegates. If a delegate yields to another delegate, the yielded delegate will come up to the podium and speak for the remaining speaking time. Note that usually if a delegate is yielded, the yielded delegates' country will be removed from the general speakers' list. Also be reminded that yielding to a second degree usually isn't in order in most conferences in Korea.

※ Note that though most conferences have similar definitions for each term, there may be slight variations from conference to conference.

7.3. Other Model UN Books & Resources

If you have read this book thoroughly, you will now know how Korea's Model UN society works and some ways to stand out among other delegates to be recognized with awards. However you may still be a bit confused on the Rules of Procedures for Model UN. That's OK. If you have never done Model UN in real life, it is almost impossible to comprehend how the rules can be applied in actual situations. That was the reason why I've tried to write a book that can draw a general picture of how Model UN works so that you will be able to absorb Model UN skills when you first go into the conference room. I tried to focus more on the general structure of Model UN and special tips that can be used in certain predicaments since these are the aspect that can't be attained simply by attending a few conferences.

With the information attained from this book, you will be off to a great start. However, I had feedback from readers who also wanted some in-depth learning on Model UN Rules of Procedures. Thus I have gathered some links to resources where you will be able to find materials made sorely for the purpose of explaining the Rules of Procedures. Links to which I have shown below are some of the best places where you can learn the rules for Model UN. If you just look thoroughly the two websites below, there really will not be much that you will *not* know about Model UN. You can of course google 'Model UN rules' and hundreds of other great sources will be available to you.

United Nations Association of the United States of America (UNA-USA) Education Materials
(http://www.unausa.org/global-classrooms-model-un/how-to-participate)

Best Delegate Institute (Model UN Company)
(http://bestdelegate.com/)

If you would like to ask me some questions about the contents of this book or rules for Model UN, then I'd be more than glad to help you. Leave a question in the Question and Answer section of the link below and I'll be able to reply in less than three days. The below link leads you to the largest Model UN online platform in Korea and since I'm one of its organizers, you will be able to get in touch with me there. A few years before I started writing this book, I wrote some Model UN tips in the Frequently Asked Question (FAQ) section and uploaded several PDF documents that I didn't put into this book due to copyright issues. Since those documents dissect the rules of procedures piece by piece, if you are interested in learning them, you can check them out through the link below.

Model UN Association of Korea: Naver Café
(http://cafe.naver.com/theworldwithus)

There were only 5 books (excluding this one) related to Model

UN of Korea that had been published as of 2015. If you would like to learn more about Model UN, you may want to look them up; although you should keep in mind that some of the following books are outdated to some extent.

All 5 books are written in Korean. Their titles in Korean are:

1. 한국청소년 모의유엔 길라잡이: 제2 반기문 도전기 (2007) / 저자 정해인 / 출판사 영비즈 / ISBN: 9788995960516 / 257쪽

This book is currently out of print and so I didn't get a chance to read it. However I've heard that the book focuses on MUNOS (the largest conference in Korea) in the context of conferences abroad. Though this book may give insights to readers on how conferences work internationally, it will not provide you with much information on how to actually prepare for one.

2. 모의 유엔회의 핸드북 (2008) / 저자 박재영 / 출판사 법문사 / ISBN: 9788918031682 / 515쪽

This book was written by a professor like an academic review. Professor Park explains how the actual United Nations procedure correlate with the Model UN procedures and how some legal issues are dealt in the United Nations. It is a comprehensive book of 515 pages that views Model UN academically.

3. 모의유엔: 글로벌 리더 만들기 프로젝트 (2011) / 저자 이종현, 김정태, 노언주, 이슬아 공저 / 출판사 하다 / ISBN: 9788997170005 / 296쪽

This book was published in 2011 and was written by some

people in an UN-related occupation and a graduate student. Although it focuses on the college circuit of Model UN, it contains some great examples that make Model UN easier to understand. The content sheds light onto the surface of Model UN. Starting delegates may gain a better understanding of Model UN through this book.

4. 모의유엔 회의 가이드북 실제와 모의 (2014) / 저자 박재영 / 출판사 법문사 / ISBN: 9788918031880 / 783쪽

This book is an updated version of the previous '모의 유엔회의 핸드북' written by professor Park. It looks into how the current Model UN proceedings are different from the actual proceeding of the UN and articulates the correct way it should be done. With a total of 783 pages, this book is a comprehensive review on Model UN and talks about different strategies to use for negotiation during session, some factors to note for the secretariats, and some tips for research on UN documents.

5. 글리스 모의유엔이 만들어진 이야기 (2015) / 저자 이원준 / 출판사 글리스 / ISBN: 9791195585809 / 304쪽

This book is about a 5 year old Model UN conference named GLIS. It talks about GLIS MUN's history and developments; however, although it has been published, it wasn't available for purchase at the time of this writing.

7.4. THIMUN Rules of Procedures

2013
Korea International Model Congress
International Committee
Rules of Procedures

Introduction and Roll Call

The Head Chair shall introduce himself and his/her Deputy Chair to the committee members. Afterwards, the Roll Call of the Committee will be conducted. With the list of the delegations in alphabetical order, the chair will read them out.

The Chair will now conduct a roll call. Delegates must answer them by raising their placards and saying either "present" or "present and voting" when their delegations are called out. Delegates who answer "present and voting" will not be able to abstain during their substantive voting procedure in this session.

For the delegates who were late and have missed the roll call, please send a note to the chair informing their arrival.

Setting the Agenda

The Chair and the Deputy Chair should decide the order of which the resolution will be debated ahead of time, after the lobbying session when all the resolution files have been collected. For KIMC 2013, there should be a minimum amount of four resolutions for each committee, except for the Security Council. After the roll call, the chair should set the agenda and the resolution to be debated.

> *The house is now in session. The first resolution to be debated will be on the question of _____. Will the main submitter please approach the podium and read out the operative clauses?*

After the main submitter reads out the operative clauses, the chair will ask if there are any points of clarification in the house. If nobody has any points of clarification in the house, the chair will set an open debate time regarding the resolution at hand. If there are any points of clarification in the house, the chair will entertain them. A point of clarification is entertained for the purpose of defining unclear grammar/vocabulary of the resolution. Question regarding the content will be entertained when the speaker accepts *points of information*.

After entertaining any points of clarification that might arise in the house, the main submitter will have 5 minutes to make her speech. After the main submitter makes her speech, the chair will ask the main submitter if he or she is open to any points of information. Main Submitters are recommended to be open to any points of information.

After POIs regarding the main submitter speech, the main submitter of the resolution may yield his/her remaining time to another delegate. Other delegates may not yield the floor to another delegate during their speeches. Thus, yielding is only allowed once per one resolution.

Debate Time

After the main submitter or the next speaker has yielded the floor back to the chair, the house is now in an open debate. The chair will entertain any delegates who raise their placards. It is crucial for the chair to recognize all delegates in order to provide fair chances for every delegate.

Points and Motions

During the debate, various points and motions can arise. These concern either the flow of the debate, or they can draw attention to a particular problem. Most points or motions can't interrupt the speaker. If a delegate wishes to make a point they should raise their placard and rise to state it. They will them be recognized by the chair. If other delegate agrees with the motion they may shout "Second!" If they not they may shout "Objection!"

If an objection was presented by a delegate, the committee has to move on to a procedural vote regarding the motion. If only seconds were held, the motion will be automatically passed. Some motions may be automatically passed due to the chair's discretion.

Here are the main points/motions used during debate.

- Point of Order
  If a mistake is made during debate by either the chair or a delegate, it is in order for a delegate to use this point.
- Point of information to the Chair

If something is unclear during debate, a delegate may direct a question to the chair using this point.
- Point of parliamentary inquiry

  If there is some sort of confusion during the debate concerning the rules of procedure, and a delegate is unsure of what to do next, he may use this point to ask the chair a question.
- Point of personal privilege

  This is the only point which is allowed to interrupt a speaker or the chair. It is used to draw attention to the discomfort of a delegate or when the delegate is not able to hear what is being said. In the latter case, a delegate would say "Point of personal privilege due to audibility"
- Point of information

  A point of information is a question to the delegate who has the floor. Pints of information always concern the content of the debate.
- Motion to move directly into voting procedure (Motion to move to the previous question)
- Motion to extend debate time

Voting Procedures

▷ Procedural Matters
1. A procedural matter is a voting on:
   a. Any motion;
   b. The invitation of a party which is not a member of

the committee.

2. Decisions of the committee on procedural matters shall be made by an affirmative vote of the *Simple Majority*. Abstentions are not in order. *A vote on procedural matters is only conducted if there are objection to the motion introduced.*

▷ Substantive Matters

1. A substantive matter is a voting on:
   a. The inclusion of an amendment;
   b. A final resolution.
2. Decision of the committee on substantive matters shall be made by an *affirmative vote of the 2/3 majority,* provided that a party to a dispute shall abstain from voting.

Course of debate

1. The main submitter reads out the operative clauses of his/her resolution.
2. The chair then sets debating time and inform the forum that is an open debate.
3. The main submitter then has the floor to explain the resolution. (Authorship speech) He/She should highlight the most important operative clauses and explain the ideas which the resolution contains.
4. When he/she has finished, the chair will 만 him whether he is open to any points of information.

He/She can reply in one of the three ways:
a. "The delegate is open to all points of information" (Opens him/herself to an unlimited number of pints of information)
b. "The delegate is open to one/two points of information" (Opens him/herself to a limited amount of points of information)
c. Says that he/she is not open to any points of information (The chair may recommend the delegate to accept at least one point of information)

5. Thereafter the delegate can yield the floor back to the chair or to another delegate.
    a. If a delegate wishes to yield the floor to another delegate (usually a co-submitter of the resolution), point 4 is repeated. However, the second delegate must yield the floor back to the chair once he/she has finished speaking.
    b. If the delegate yields the floor back to the chair, the chair will then yield the floor to another delegate and points 4 and 5 are repeated.
    c. Only main submitters are allowed to yield their remaining time to another delegate. This is also limited to their remaining time after their 5 minute authorship speech. Even if he/she is the main submitter, he/she can't yield his/her remaining time to another delegate during the debate; he/she can only yield after his/her authorship speech.

6. When the debating time for the resolution has elapsed, all delegate vote on the resolution. Delegates can vote in favor or against, or they can abstain.

Amendments

1. Amendments can only be submitted by a speaker who has the floor.
2. An amendment is only in order if it is submitted to the chair on the official amendment sheet before the delegate takes the floor. It must be easily legible.
3. The chair reads it out for all delegates to note down.
4. Every amendment (approved ones) will always be debated and put to vote.
5. Closed debate for amendments (for/against) will be in order.
6. Only one amendment (max: one per entire clause) per amendment sheet will be in entertained.
7. Chair should prioritize constructive amendments, e.g. adding a clause.
8. On an amendment, delegates can only vote for, against, or abstain.
9. Amendments to the second degree is not in order in KIMC 2013.

Plenary Session

There is a plenary session at the end of the last day;

all committee delegates join together in the same conference room for a general debate. Committee chairs must choose each committee's representative resolution (1 per committee) of their committees and submit the resolution to the Secretary General before the plenary session. The chosen resolutions will be put into debate in the plenary session. Security Council's resolution will be discussed first, and the session will continue to debate in alphabetical order. (ex: SC→SP1→SP2→UNCCC →…) All resolution will be printed and handed out to every participants of the conference; all delegates have equal rights to make speeches, POIs, and votes.

The purpose of the plenary session is to pass or fail the representative resolutions of each committee. The course of debate will be the same as that of the individual committees. Note passing however, will not be in order.

7.5. UNA-USA Rules of Procedures

SIGMUN
Rules of Procedures

1. Organization

Clause 1 | Secretariat

1. The Secretariat team is divided into the following departments:
   a. Secretary General
   b. Standing Advisor
   c. Deputy Secretary General
   d. Department of Conference Management
   e. Department of Conference Education
   f. Department of Conference Training
   g. Department of Public Relations
2. The members of the Secretariat may issue either written or oral statements at any time during the committee sessions.

3. All members of the Secretariat must report to and receive guidelines from the Secretary General, the chief exective.

Clause 2 | Student Officer

1. Student officers are divided into:
   a. Head chairs
   b. Deputy chairs
2. Student officers have responsibilities such as:
   a. Opening nad closing of each session
   b. Porposal and enforcement of all the Rules of Procedures within their respective committees
   c. Imposition of time restraints on all motions and committee proceedings
   d. Involvement of award consideration in their respective committees
3. All student officres receive guidance and instruction from the Department of Conference Education.
4. All student officers must report to and receive guidelines from all Secretariats.

Clause 3 | Administrative Staff

1. Administrative staffs are divided into:
   a. Secretariat staff
   b. Head staff
   c. Staff (Committee)

2. Administrative staff have responsibilities such as:
   a. Note passing and screening
   b. Helping respective committees in logistical manners
   c. Night guard
3. All administrative staffs receive guidance and instructions from the Department of Conference Training.
4. All administrative staff must report to and receive guidelines from all Secretariats.

Clause 4 | Participants

1. Participants of the conference are referred to as 'delegates' and are responsible for formal involvement in the debate, representing the prespective nations they are assigned.
2. Participants are considered to be the delegate of a specific committee involved in the United Nations, serving as diplomats of each representing nation.

2. General Rules and Ethics

Clause 1 | Language

1. Englih is the only language allowed in all English committee sessions, including announcements, speeches, notes, and resolutions.
2. Delegates wishing to use other languages to communicate must receive permission from the Secretariat.

3. The English only language policy is flexible to only the follwing:
   a. Between the members of the Secretariat
   b. Between the members of the Secretariat and the student oficers
   c. Between the members of the Secretariat and the administrative staff
   d. Between non-members of SIGMN
   e. Unofficial communication when committees are not in session
4. Participants that constantly break the English only language policy after constant warning will be removed from award consideration and/or certificates of participation.

Clause 2 | Electronic Communication Devices

1. The use of laptop computers, cell phones, and any other electronic devices will not be allowed during committee sessions uncless specifically approved by the student officers or members of the Secretariat.
2. Under chairs' discretion, delegates may use electronic devices solely for the purpose of researching material and writing resolutoins.
3. Electronic devices may be used when the committee is not in session outside of the committee room for purposes that are not related to the conference.

Clause 3 | Alcohol and Tobacco

1. All participants of the conference, including student officres, administrative staffs, and delegates, are strictly prohibited intake of alcohol or smoke in any and all circumstances during the conference, regardless of ages.
2. Any student officres, administrative staffs, or delegates that impeach these rules must follow instruction given by the members of the Secretariat regarding punishment are subject to all of the following consequences:
   a. Temporary or permanent expulsion
   b. Confiscation of the prohibited items
   c. Direct report to the participatn's parents or guardians
   d. Direct report to the participant's school authorities

Clause 4 | Sexual Harassment

1. Sexual harrassment of any kind is prohibited.
2. Incidents of sexual harrassment should be reported to the Secretariat immediately.
3. Any student officers, administrative staffs, or delegates that impeach these rules must follow instructions given b the members of the Secretariat regarding punishment are subject to all of the following consequences:
   a. Temporary or permanent expulsion
   b. Confiscation of the prohibited items
   c. Direct report to the participatn's parents or guardians
   d. Direct report to the participant's school authorities

Clause 5 | Relationship Between Participants

1. Student officers and administrative staffs must behave professionally toward delegates.
2. Student officers and administrative staffs must not reveal any confidential information during char or administrative staff training sessions about the conferece to delegates.
3. As representatives of countries or organizations, delegates must respect all other delegates, student officers, administrative staffs, and the Secretariats.
4. All participants must maintain relationships in accordance to their positions and are prohibited from any private relationships or conversations during the conference.
5. Delegates are strictly prohibited from bribing the student officers or the Secretariat, especially in areas of conference proceedings and award considerations.

Clause 6 | Absences and Quorum

1. Any delegates who miss more than two sessions of the conference will not be qualified to receive their certificate of participation unless their absence has been notified to the Secretariat and given approval prior to the sessions.
2. Student officers may only declare a committee to have met the quorum and permit proceeding of the debate when at least two-thirds of the delegates participating in a committee is present.
3. Student officers must keep track of the number of

delegates present in the committee room before conducting a voting procedure to ensure the committee has met the quorum.

Clause 7 | Entry and Exit

1. Delegate cannot leave the committee room for more than 20 minutes during the session unless given approval by student officers or the Secretairats.
2. Delegates leaving the committee room must hand over their name tags to the administrative staff to confirm their leaving.
3. Because committee rooms are secured during voting procedure, any delegates outside the committee room during voting procedures cannot vote.
4. Student officers and delegate may not enter any other room except their assigned committees that they belong to unless they are given approval by the Secretariat.

Clause 8 | Dress Code

1. All participants of the conference must adhere to the following dress code: Western business attire.
2. T-shirs, sweatshirts, jeans, shrts, sneakers, sandals, filp-flops, open-toe shoes, or any other kind of informal wear are strictly prohibited.
3. The dress code is in effect from the official opening of the conference to the official closing of the conference.

4. Participants that fail to abide to the dress code will receive warning from the Secretariat and may not be permitted to enter the committee room.

Clause 9 | Plagiarism

1. All written work publicly displayed for the purpose of the conference, especially resolution and amendments, must not be plagiarized in any shape or form.
2. All written material drafted before the conference, including chair reports and position papers, must include citations, if referenced from other sources.
3. If any work is found to impeach this rule, student officres will be dismissed from their positions and delegates will be exempted from award considerations and participation certificates.
4. The Secretariats have the final decision regarding plagiarism and may adjudicate violations of these rules.

Clause 10 | Emergency Situation

1. In the case of an emergency, student officers are responsible for directing delegates under the directions and guidance of the Secretiarts.
2. Members of the Secretariat have the right to override official Rules of Procedure in time of emergency.
3. Participatns of the conference must follow the dirctions and guidance of the Secretariat in times of emergency.

Clause 11 | Preparation Prior to the Conference

1. Delegates are required to have one prewritten opening speech prior to the conference, the speech a duration of 60 seconds or less.
2. Delegates are not required to write position papers in preparation of the conference, but are highly suggested in order to help their understanding and widen prior knowledge of the issues that will be discussed within the committee rooms.
3. Prewritten resolutions are strictly prohibited and delegates found with evidence of prewritten resolutions will be exempted from award consideration and participation certificates.

Clause 12 | Registration

1. The participation fee is announced via the SIGMUN official site or Facebook page
2. Registration is only confirmed with committee and counry assignments via email when payment is completed.

3. General Committee Proceedings

Clause 1 | Roll Call

1. The committee session begins with a roll call. When the chairs calls out the delegations in alphabetical order, all

delegates should raise their placards high and say either present or present and voting.
2. Any delegates entering the conference room late need to send a note to the chairs notifying whether they are present or present and voting, or their votes will not be counted during the voting procedure and their attendance will not be recognized.
3. If the quorum is not met, the chair annot declair committee into session and is obliged to contact the Secretairats.

Clause 2 | Setting the Agenda

1. When there is no agenda item on the floor, the committee has to set the agenda through a motion to set the agenda.
2. A motion to set the agenda is entertained by the chairs when a delegate raises a motion to set the agenda to agenda item A.
3. After hearing this motion, chairs will open a limited speaker's list on the motion to set the agenda and entertain two delegates to speak for and two delegates to speak against the motion, the speech a duration of 60 seconds or less.
4. After the speakers' list is exhausted, the chairs should move directly into a procedural voting procedure, which requires a simple majority to pass.
5. If the motion fails, the committee will automatically move onto the next agenda without additional motions to set the

agenda.

Clause 3 | Speakers' List

1. Once an agenda item is determined, the chairs will open a general speakers' list and entertain any delegates wishing to express their opinions pertaining to the agenda.
2. The speakers' list for the general debate continues as resolutions are introduced as well, unless a limited speakers' list takes place for motions or amendments.
3. Delegates may be added to the speakers' list by raising their placards to get recognized when the chairs open the speakers' list, or by sending a note to the chairs requesting to be placed on the speakers' list.
4. Chairs may accept motions or points during the speakers' list, but only when a speaker is not speaking on the podium, with the exception of points of personal privilege.
5. The time for speeches on the speakers' list is automatically set to 90 seconds at the beginning of the session, but can be adjusted by chairs' discretion or through a motion to set the speakers' time.
6. Delegates may not approach the podium unless recognized by the chairs.
7. Delegates may not go back to their seats from the podium unless recognized by the chairs.

Clause 4 | Speeches

1. Delegates are forbidden to use first person pronouns and second person pronouns, such as I, you, or we, since they are representing not themselves but countries or organizations. When referring to their delegation, the delegates must refer to themselves with third person pronouns, such as he, she, or the delegate of A.
2. Delegates on the speakers' list may yield their remaining time to:
    a. Points of information:
        i. Points of information must be concise and must be in a question format.
        ii. It is only considered using remaining time when the delegate on the podium is answering a point of information.
        iii. Follow ups are granted upon request and under chairs' discretion.
        iv. The delegate on the podium may choose to answer the question on the podium or reply after going back to his or her seat in note form.
        v. Direct conversation between the delegates is not in order, as so, if the delegate on the podium has difficulty understanding the question, he or she must ask the chairs to request the delegate asking the question to rephrase the question.
    b. Another delegates:
        i. A delegate may not yield the remaining time to another delegate who is not a sponsor to during an

authorship speech when introducing a resolution.
  ii. Yielding to the second degree is not in order.
  iii. A delegate can yield to another delegate only if the remaining time exceeds 30 seconds.
  iv. No delegate may refuse the yield given to him or her whenever the action has taken place even if the delegates
  v. Delegates do not have to continue speaking on the same ideas as the delegate that yielded the floor to him or her
 c. Chair
  i. Delegate may yield the remaining time back to the chairs.
  ii. The chairs will tell the delegates to return back to his or her seat to end his or her speech when yielded the remaining time.
2. Delegates should adhere to the time limitations, and the chairs have the authority to suspend their speech once it exceeds time:
 a. Chairs will notify the delegates to come to their closing remarks when 10 seconds are remaining.
 b. When the speakers' time elapses, chairs may completely stop the speaker on the podium and ask the speaker to return back to his or her designated seat.

4. Points and Motions

Clause 1 | Point of Order

1. A point of order is raised by delegates when the delegates notice an error in the chairs' parliamentary procedures during the discussion of any matter.
2. Chairs may rule the point of order out under their discretion.
3. A point of order may not interrupt another speaker.

Clause 2 | Point of Personal Privilege

1. A point of personal privilege is raised by delegates when delegates experience personal discomfort to request the discomfort to be resolved, such as audibility or room temperature.
2. A point of personal privilege may interrupt a speaker only for audibility issues.
3. For any other discomfort, a point of personal privilege may not interrupt another speaker.

Clause 3 | Point of Parliamentary Inquiry

1. A point of parliamentary inquiry is raised by delegates when delegates wish to ask the chairs a question regarding the Rules of Procedure.
2. A point of parliamentary inquiry may not interrupt another speaker.

Clause 4 | Point of Clarification

1. A point of clarification is raised by delegates after one of the sponsors of a resolution, after the draft resolution is approved by the chairs, reads out the operative clauses, to ask a question regarding clarification of terms.
2. A point of clarification is different in nature from a point of information, as:
   a. It is only allowed for delegates to rectify confusion from the speech or the resolution resulting from confusing terms or word concepts, such as the names for a committee.
   b. If a point of clarification is made in an argumentative nature and resembles a point of information, the point will directly be ruled out of order by the chairs.
3. A point of parliamentary inquiry may not interrupt another speaker.

Clause 5 | Point of Notice

1. The chairs of the committee may intervene during debate at any point and issue a point of notice.
2. This point can be delivered either through note form or in oral form during the debate to a member who is clearly and persistently out of order or is misrepresenting the foreign policy of the country he or she is representing.
3. This point of notice serves as a warning to the delegate it pertains to, and thus consecutive offences will be

reported to the Secretariat.
4. A point of parliamentary inquiry may not interrupt another speaker.

Clause 6 | Motion to Move Into Unmoderated Caucus

1. A motion to move into unmoderated caucus is called when a delegate wishes to move around within the committee room and share his or her opinion on resolutions, amendments, or agenda items or to receive signatories for his or her resolutions or amendments.
2. A motion to move into unmoderated caucus must specify the specific time and purpose.
3. The maximum time limit for unmoderated caucuses is 20 minutes. An unmoderated caucus cannot end unless the specified time passes.
4. Under chairs' discretion, time for an unmoderated caucus may be adjusted.
5. This motion to move into unmoderated caucus is a procedural vote that requires a simple majority to pass.
6. Speeches on the podium are not allowed during an unmoderated caucus.

Clause 7 | Motion to Move Into Moderated Caucus

1. A motion to move into moderated caucus is called when a delegate wishes to temporarily suspend the general or limited speakers' list and proceed with the debate by

recognizing delegates one by one from their seats.
2. The speeches made within a moderated caucus within the individual speaking time must pertain to the purpose mentioned in the motion. No yielding is allowed.
3. A motion to move into moderated caucus must specify the specific time, purpose, and individual speaking time. The overall time duration of the moderated caucus should be the multiples of the individual speaking time.
4. The maximum time limit for moderated caucuses is 30 minutes. A moderated caucus cannot end unless the specified time passes.
5. Under chairs' discretion, time for a moderated caucus may be adjusted.
6. The motion to move into moderated caucus is a procedural vote that requires a simple majority to pass.

Clause 8 | Motion to Table Debate on the Resolution, Amendment, or Agenda Item

1. A motion to table debate on the resolution, amendment, or agenda item is called when a delegate wishes to temporarily pause debate on the resolution, amendment, or agenda item to move to the next resolution, amendment, or agenda item.
2. Upon receiving this motion, the chairs will entertain two speakers for and two speakers against the motion with individual speaking time of 60 seconds by opening a

limited speakers' list on this motion. No yielding is allowed.

3. This motion to table debate on the resolution, amendment, or agenda item is a procedural vote that requires a super majority to pass.
4. If the motion passes, no further discussion or action on the resolution, amendment, or agenda item tabled is to take place until a motion to resume debate on this issue is raised.
5. A motion to table debate on the resolution is out of order when the committee is in the middle of discussing an amendment for that resolution.

Clause 9 | Motion to Resume Debate on the Resolution, Amendment, or Agenda Item

1. A motion to resume debate on the resolution, amendment, or agenda item is called when a delegate wishes to bring back debate on the resolution, amendment, or agenda item that was tabled in a previous motion to table the debate.
2. Upon receiving this motion, the chairs will entertain two speakers and two speakers against the motion with individual speaking time of 60 seconds by opening a limited speakers' list on this motion. No yielding is allowed.
3. This motion to resume debate on the resolution, amendment, or agenda item is a procedural vote that

requires a super majority to pass.
4. If the motion passes, the resolution or amendment is resumed back to the floor once more, allowing further discussion or action on that specific item to take place.
5. Resuming debate on an agenda item can only be done by a motion to set the agenda. This motion is only in order when the committee has no agenda item on the floor. Furthermore, the agenda item that has not been discussed in the committee before can only be set by a motion to set the agenda.
6. A motion to resume debate on the resolution is out of order when the committee is in the middle of discussing an amendment for another resolution.

Clause 10 | Motion to Close Debate on the Resolution, Amendment, or Agenda Item

1. A motion to close debate on the resolution, amendment, or agenda item is raised when a delegate wishes to close debate on an item that is fully debated on.
2. Upon receiving this motion, the chairs will entertain two speakers against the motion with individual speaking time of 60 seconds by opening a limited speakers' list on this motion. No yielding is allowed.
3. This motion to close debate on the resolution, amendment, or agenda item is a procedural vote that requires a super majority to pass.

4. The chairs may rule out the motion, and the chairs' decision cannot be appealed.
5. If the motion passes, the committee will directly move into voting procedures on the resolution or amendment.
6. When a motion to close debate on an agenda item is passed, all resolutions pertaining to the agenda item is put into immediate vote, in order as the serial number dictates. Delegates may also raise a motion to change the order of voting on resolutions if they wish to do so.
   a. In SIGMUN, passing of multiple resolutions is allowed.

Clause 11 | Motion to Adjourn the Session

1. A motion to adjourn the session can be raised if the remaining time of the session does not exceed 30 minutes.
2. A motion to adjourn the session must specify the specific time of resumption and purpose.
3. This motion to adjourn the session is a procedural vote that requires a super majority to pass.
4. Under chairs' discretion and under consideration of quality of debate, the chairs may rule out this motion.

Clause 12 | Motion to Adjourn the Meeting

1. A motion to adjourn the meeting can be raised if the remaining time of the session does not exceed 30 minutes and if the current session is the last session of the last

day.
2. A motion to adjourn the session must specify the specific time of resumption and purpose.
3. This motion to adjourn the session is a procedural vote that requires a super majority to pass.
4. Under chairs' discretion and under consideration of quality of debate, the chairs may rule out this motion.

Clause 13 | Motion to Modify Speaking Time

1. A motion to modify the speaking time is called when a delegate believes that the individual speaking time preset before the debate of 90 seconds is either too long or too short and wish to change the individual speaking time.
2. This motion to modify speaking time is directly put into vote and is a procedural vote that requires a simple majority to pass.
3. If the chairs consider the modification to speaking time an interfering factor to the flow of the overall debate, the chairs may rule the motion out of order or change the suggested individual speaking time with chairs' discretion.
4. The modified speaking time is reset to 90 seconds at the beginning of each session.

Clause 14 | Motion to Move Into Voting Procedures on the Resolution or Amendment

1. A motion to move into voting procedures on the resolution or amendment is called when a delegate believes that there has been adequate time spent on debate on the resolution or amendment and wish to vote on it.
2. This motion to move into voting procedures on the resolution or amendment is directly put into vote and is a procedural vote that requires a simple majority to pass.
3. Under chairs' discretion and under consideration of quality of debate, the chairs may rule out this motion.

Clause 15 | Motion to Vote by Clause

1. A motion to vote by clause is called when a delegate believes that it would be more beneficial to vote on the draft resolution in a clause by clause format, after recognizing that not all clauses in the draft resolution are needed.
2. A motion to vote by clause can only be raised after a motion to move into voting procedures on the draft resolution is passed.
3. This motion to vote by clause is directly put into vote and is a procedural vote that requires a simple majority to pass.
4. Under chairs' discretion and under consideration of quality of debate, the chairs may rule out this motion.

Clause 16 | Motion to Reorder the Voting for Resolutions

1. A motion to reorder the voting for resolutions is called when a delegate believes that it would be more beneficial for the resolution he or she is a sponsor of to be voted on earlier than another resolution.
2. This motion to vote by clause is directly put into vote and is a procedural vote that requires a simple majority to pass.
3. Under chairs' discretion and under consideration of quality of debate, the chairs may rule out this motion.

Clause 17 | Motion to Suspend Rules

1. A motion to suspend rules is called when a delegate believes that the committee is in circumstances in which adherence to the Rules of Procedure hampers proceedings.
2. A motion to suspend rules requires the delegate wishing to raise the motion to indicate specifically which rule he or she wants suspended, for what purpose, and for what duration of time.
3. This motion to suspend rules is directly put into vote and is a procedural vote that requires a super majority to pass.
4. Before implementing this motion, chairs must seek approval from the Secretariat.

Clause 18 | Right of Reply

1. When delegates feel like their national integrity has been

impugned by other delegates, they ma submit a Right of Reply through note form to the chairs.
2. Chairs will grant the Right of Reply under their discretion and will send a note back to the delegate if approved, and the delegate will be granted to speak for 60 seconds.
3. Time remaining after a Right of Reply cannot be yielded to another delegate or Points of Information.
4. A Right of Reply to the second degree is not allowed.

Clause 19 | Appeal

1. When a delegate believes that the chairs' ruling is inappropriate, he or she may appeal to the decision of the chairs by writing a note to the Secretariat, with clear indication that the note is an appeal.
2. The delegate must pass the note to an administrative staff of his or her respective committee and request the note to be sent directly to the Secretariat.
3. The members of the Secretariat will adjudicate the appeal and render a decision.

5. Resolutions and Amendments

Clause 1 | Resolutions

1. A resolution is the work of the delegates within a committee that contains solutions for the agenda item.

2. A resolution is divided into two parts:
   a. Preambulatory clauses, which:
      i   Only include facts about the agenda
      ii Cannot be amended
   b. Operative clauses, which:
      i. Contain actions to be taken to solve the issue
      ii. Contain specific information divided into subclauses and sub-subclauses
      iii. Can be amended
3. Multiple resolutions can be introduced and remain on the floor, but they all have to pertain to the agenda item on the floor.
4. Resolutions will temporarily be put aside from the floor when amendments or procedural debates take precedence.
5. Below is the process of introducing a resolution:
   a. Delegates should write a resolution with other delegates and receive signatories and sponsors, which must exceed onethird of the delegates present in the committee.
   b. Delegates can submit resolutions to the chairs by sending their USB through the administrative staff during formal debate or directly to chairs during informal debate in unmoderated caucuses.
   c. Chairs will revise the formats and content regarding plagiarism, relevance to the agenda, and division with other resolutions on the floor. Chairs will give the resolution a serial number in the order of committee,

agenda item, and resolution number. (ex. UNHRC-A-1, UNHRC, Agenda Item A, Resolution #1)

    d. The administrative staff will deliver the USB to the Approval Panel, who will then return it after examination to the administrative staff.

    e. The administrative staff will make copies and distribute them to all delegates and chairs.

    f. The debate is closed with a motion to close debate on the resolution, with two speakers against the motion.

    g. When the motion to close debate on the resolution passes, the committee will move directly into the substantive voting procedures of the resolution itself.

        i. The resolution requires a super majority to pass.

        ii. Abstentions are allowed.

    h. After the resolution passes, clapping is in order.

6. The content of the resolutions cannot be mentioned nor discussed prior to their introduction in any committee's substantive speeches.

7. Drafting a complete resolution in advance to the conference is strictly prohibited, and doing so will result in an automatic expulsion from award considerations and participation certificates.

Clause 2 | Introducing Draft Resolutions

1. In order to introduce a resolution to the committee, the delegate must complete the following steps:

a. The requisite number of signatories and sponsors must be met on the resolution:
   i. The requisite number will be one-third of the delegates present in the committee.
   ii. Being a signatory of the resolution does not imply in any means that the delegate is a supporter of the resolution, but rather means that he or she wishes to discuss the resolution in the committee.
b. A resolution should have sponsors. There are no main submitters in SIGMUN 2015.
c. A draft resolution may be introduced when the chairs approve it:
   i. Delegates should submit the draft resolution to the chairs either through the administrative staff or directly during informal debate for approval.
   ii. Delegates should wait until the chairs notifies back until the draft resolution is copied and distributed after approval.
d. When the floor is open, a sponsor of the draft resolution may raise a motion to introduce the draft resolution, referring to the resolution with its serial number, given by the chairs through note form when approving the resolution.
e. A sponsoring nation who has raised the motion will approach the podium and read out the operative clauses.
f. After the delegate reads out the operative clauses of the

resolution, the chairs will entertain point of clarifications from the committee.
g. The delegate may give an optional authorship speech of the resolution with a maximum time limit of 5 minutes.
h. After the authorship speech, the chairs will entertain points of information from the committee. The remaining time can be used to yield to another sponsor or delegate or yield back to the chair.
i. The draft resolution is then considered formally introduced to the committee and is open to discussion and reference during committee session.
2. More than one draft resolution may be introduced at the same time as long as they are within the same agenda.
3. The introduced draft resolution on the floor may be discussed continuously until the committee tables or closes debate or introduces an amendment.
4. No individual owns any documents that are produced. All the documents are considered property of SIGMUN.

Clause 3 | Approving Draft Resolutions

1. The chairs of the committee will check the draft resolution for the following:
   a. The number of requisite signatories of the resolution
   b. Relevance to the committee's current agenda item
   c. General quality of the draft resolution

    d. Distinct difference from prior resolutions in the approval process

    e. Adherence to the resolution formatting guideline

    f. File format of word document (.doc or .docx)

2. The chairs will assign a serial number after reviewing the categories mentioned above in order of resolution approval by the chairs on the agenda item.

Clause 4 | Amendments

1. An amendment is a possible alteration to the meaning or intentions of a particular clause in the draft resolution on the floor, which must be voted upon by the delegates within the committee before the amendment becomes effective.

    a. Preambulatory clauses of the resolution may not be amended.

    b. Only one action can be taken at a time in one amendment.

2. Below is the process of introducing a amendment:

    a. All amendments must be sent to the chairs and approved by the chairs through note form.

    b. When an amendment to a resolution is introduced, the general speakers' list is suspended temporarily.

    c. After the chair reads out the amendment, a limited speakers' list on the amendment will be open for speakers for and against speakers of the amendment.

i. All speeches must remain relevant to the amendment itself.
   ii. Yields to points of information or yields to another delegate are allowed at this time.
  d. The debate is closed with a motion to close debate on the amendment, with two speakers against the motion.
  e. When the motion to close debate on the amendment passes, the committee will move directly into the substantive voting procedures of the amendment itself.
   i. The amendment requires a super majority to pass.
   ii. Abstentions are allowed.
  f. After the amendment passes, the chairs will reread the amendment and inform the committee to make the corresponding changes to the resolution.
3. After substantive voting on the amendment, the temporarily suspended general speakers' list is resumed.
4. There are no friendly amendments nor amendments to the second degree in SIGMUN.

Clause 5 | Introducing Amendments

1. In order to introduce an amendment to the committee, the delegate must complete the following steps:
  a. The delegate must obtain the approval of the chair through note form prior to its introduction.
  b. A delegate is allowed to raise a motion to introduce an amendment to the resolution currently being debated

on whenever the floor is open.
  i. Amendments without the chairs' approval or amendments with irrelevant content to the resolution are not in order.
  ii. All motions, including the motion to introduce an amendment, will be voted upon following the order of precedence.
  iii. Under chairs' discretion, any amendment may be ruled out of order.
c. When a delegate raises a motion to introduce an amendment, the motion is directly in order under chairs' discretion.
d. After the motion is made, the chair will read out the amendment and the delegate who raised the motion will approach the podium.
e. The delegate shall receive points of clarification regarding the amendment from the committee. The only case when points of clarification are not entertained is when the amendment is to strike a clause.
f. The delegate may give an optional authorship speech of the amendment with a maximum time limit of 2 minutes.
g. After the authorship speech, the chairs will entertain points of information from the committee. The remaining time can be used to yield to another sponsor or delegate or yield back to the chair.
h. The amendment is then considered formally introduced

to the committee and is open to discussion and reference during the debate time for the amendment.
2. Only one amendment can be on the floor at a time.
3. When two or more amendments are proposed at the same time, the chairs will discuss which amendment generates the greatest impact to the resolution.
4. No individual owns any documents that are produced. All the documents are considered property of SIGMUN.

Clause 6 | Approving Amendments

1. The chairs shall approve amendments with the same manner and procedure as for resolutions except the process with the Approval Panel.
2. The serial number on an amendment shall be made by adding a number to the serial number for the resolution the amendment pertains to.

6. Voting Procedures

Clause 1 | Procedural Vote

1. A procedural vote is any vote on procedural matters such as motions.
2. This vote is conducted by delegates raising placards, administrative staff counting votes, and chairs announcing results of the voting procedure.

3. For procedural voting procedure, delegates may vote:
   a. For
   b. Against
4. A motion that requires a simple majority passes when the votes for exceed half the delegates present in the committee.
5. A motion that requires a two-thirds majority, or a super majority, passes when the votes for exceed or is equal to two-thirds of the delegates present in the committee.
6. Delegates representing countries may vote.

Clause 2 | Substantive Vote

1. A substantive vote is a vote on substantive matters such as resolutions and amendments.
2. This vote is conducted by delegates raising placards, administrative staff counting votes, and chairs announcing results of the voting procedure.
3. For substantive voting procedure, delegates may vote:
   a. For
   b. Against
   c. Abstain
4. This vote requires a two-thirds majority, or a super majority, to pass.
5. After voting procedures have been conducted and the results of the voting announced, the chairs will continue proceeding on with the session.

Clause 3 | Voting Procedure on Motions

1. No seconds or objections exist in the Rules of Procedure of SIGMUN.
2. The passing and failing of all motions will be determined by a voting process, following the order of precedence.

7. Order of Precedence

Clause 1 | Order of Precedence

1. All points and motions take the following precedence:
   a. Point of Personal Privilege
   b. Point of Order
   c. Point of Parliamentary Inquiry
   d. Point of Notice
   e. Motion to Suspend Rules
   f. Motion for a Roll Call Vote
   g. Motion to Adjourn the Session
   h. Motion to Adjourn the Meeting
   i. Motion to Modify Speaking Time
   j. Motion to Move Into Unmoderated Caucus
   k. Motion to Move Into Moderated Caucus
   l. Motion to Introduce Draft Resolution
   m. Motion to Introduce Amendment
   n. Motion to Table Debate
      A. Motion to Resume Debate
   o. Motion to Close Debate

2. Within points and motions, one that casts greater effect on the debate takes precedence.
3. Within the same motions, one that has the longer duration takes precedence.
4. Within the same points, one that is introduced prior takes precedence.

Clause 2 | Order of Precedence at the Beginning of Voting Procedure

1. At the beginning of the voting procedure, the following points and motions are in order with the following order of precedence:
   a. Point of Personal Privilege
   b. Point of Order
   c. Point of Parliamentary Inquiry
   d. Motion for a Roll Call Vote

English Committee Rules of Procedures, Created by SIGMUN Secretariat
Content from —
SIGMUN 2014 | Department of Conference Education, Yeonjun Sung
SIGMUN THE WINTER | Standing Advisor, Sang-Yup Lee
SIGMUN THE THIRD | Department of Conference Education, Serim Jang

7.6. Model UN research paper

Lastly, the following resource is one of the few research papers that deals with Korea's Model UN society. It is a study published by the Infornomics Society during the 2015 London International Conference on Education. This paper would provide you with the general background on Korean Model UN society's history and developments.

Exploring Model UN in Korea: Its History and Developments

John Sang-Yup Lee
Global Vision Christian School, Republic of Korea

Abstract

Model UN in Korea has developed rapidly since its start in 1959. Nowadays about 30 national Model UN conferences are held in Korea and numerous organizations including school clubs host countless mini-conferences. Though only a small percentage of students were able to attend conferences in the past due to varying reasons, efforts have been made to combat those problems. The current problem is that as no one had researched and documented Korea's Model UN society, its history of developments are fading without any note in the knowledge domain. Therefore this research was made to document diverse aspects of Korea's high school Model

UN society for the first time in order to shed light into its structures. By doing so, this paper aims to help provide background knowledge for educators to have more faculties in dealing with the subject of Model UN.

1. Introduction

After 1990s, with Korea's sixth and seventh national curriculums to direct education appropriate for the globalized world, English education in Korea focused on English's communicative competence; debate competitions became prevalent and an activity called Model United Nations (MUN) widespread. But while Model UN is sometimes utilized even as a school subject abroad, it hasn't been studied much in Korea yet. Thus to get to know what Model UN is and how it has been operating in Korea, this research was designed to provide background knowledge about Korea's Model UN society. (Note that as there hadn't been any previous research conducted in this area, this study is largely based on the author's 4 years of research in the field).

The Beginning of Model UN

Model UN is one of the largest student activities in the world. In a Model UN conference, 100~1000 students gather for 1~4 days to discuss each committee agendas under the perspective of each assigned country. Through Model UN, students learn to perform extensive academic research in different fields according to respective committee agendas. Students also learn how to make public speeches and learn to work with one another to construct resolutions. Model UN's educational value is corroborated by Johnson as he states that Model UN environment formulates cooperative learning that generates higher achievement for students-both academically and socially [3].

Although a program named Model League of Nations started before the United Nations was formed in 1945, Model League of Nations became Model United Nations in 1947 and has spread internationally as an educational tool [5].

Worldwide, World Federation of United Nations Association (WFUNA) and organizations like the United States of America-United Nations Association (UNA-USA) now take leading roles in promoting Model UN. Both organizations sponsor numerous Model UN conferences and related education programs; in Korea, Kyunghee University is in affiliation with both WFUNA and UNA-USA. It hosts Model UN camps and a conference which is called Global Classroom: Seoul (GC: Seoul) [4].

Model UN in Korea

The first Model UN conference in Korea dates back to 1959 when Hankuk University of Foreign Studies (HUFS) organized its first HUFS International Model UN (HIMUN) for college students on the agenda of UN Disarmament [8]. The United Nations Association-Republic of Korea (UNA-ROK) also hosted its first conference named National Model UN-Korea (NMUN-Korea) with the Korea University in 1995. 25 universities with 200 students participated in this event [7].

As can be seen above, Model UN in Korea had initially developed in Korea's university circuit. However starting from 2004, high school students also started to participate in Model UN. The first high school Model UN conference was Model United Nations of Seoul (MUNOS) hosted by a company called Chosun Education. Though the first MUNOS had only 70 participants, more students started to participate overtime. In 2007 when interests in the UN rose in Korea with the selection of Ki-Moon Ban as UN's Secretary General, over 500 students participated in the fourth MUNOS [6].

High school students also started to organize Model UN conferences from 2010 for themselves; one of those includes GLIS Model UN that started with 300 participants [1].

2. Analysis

2.1. Developments during 2000~2009

To analyze Korea's Model UN society before 2010, the year when high school students started to make conferences for themselves, having access to documented sources would be essential. However, currently there are only fragmented sources that simply imply the expansion of Model UN in the university circuit; UNA-ROK website states that while only 150 students from 38 colleges participated in its 6th NMUN-Korea conference held in 2000, 420 students from 55 colleges participated in its 15th conference held in 2009 [7]. If the number of university students who attended other college conferences such as HIMUN is counted, the total number of college students' participation in a year would reach at least 1,000 students before 2010.

Indeed, MUNOS conference which high school students participate did exist since 2004. But almost all other existing conferences were aimed for university students before 2010. High school students that did participate in Model UN conference were limited to only 100~500 students who attended elite schools such as foreign language high schools [6]. Thus it can be said that while the 10 years after year 2000 was a time for Model UN to spread throughout South Korea, it was largely limited to the university circuit.

Note that in 2007 a Model UN book called 'MUNOS' was published by its Secretary General and Deputy Secretary General. But because the book's content was limited solely to the history of MUNOS conference itself, it was not considered as a documented research on Korea's overall Model UN society in this paper.

2.2. Developments after 2010

2.2.1. Region

From here on, this paper would focus on the high school circuit of Model UN society in Korea. This is because the author had focused his research in high school Model UN circuit and as high school Model UN pool had become larger than the college pool after 2010.

To begin, year 2010 was when Model UN became accessible enough for high school students to also organize a conference for themselves. While Model UN conferences were initially hosted by universities and companies, Model UN such as GLIS MUN was organized by high school students in 2010 [1]. Starting from 2011, high school Model UN unions also began to form and Korea International Model Congress (KIMC) Union became the largest union with over 30 member schools [2].

To view Model UN under regional perspective, the expansion of Model UN first took its place in Seoul, the capital of South Korea. All Model UN conferences including MUNOS, GLIS MUN, KIMC Union, NMUN-Korea, and HIMUN initially took place in Seoul. This may be because the official language for Model UN was initially set in English (conferences started using Korean as its official language only after 2012~13) and only a portion of students that were educated enough to use the language fluently were able to participate. And because most students with that amount of foreign language education lived in Seoul, conferences were able to expand from Seoul.

As time went, Model UN have spread to other regions in Korea such as Jeju Island, Incheon, Busan, and many more as shown in Figure 1 below. Students who wanted to gain English communication competence began to join the conference and the pool was able to widen itself.

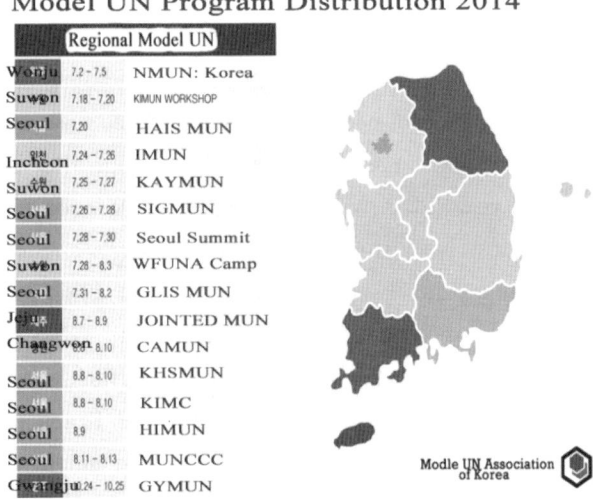

Figure 1. Model UN distribution in Korea
Note: A colored version of figure 1 can be found in p. 49 of this book.

2.2.2. Participation

Region is an important factor to consider in analyzing the trend of participants since if one lives far away from the conference venue, one would not likely participate. However, factors regarding the conference itself also determine whether a student would participate in a specific conference or not. 2.2.2. will focus on those factors in order to see the development of Korea's Model UN society.

Firstly, the rules of Model UN make students decide whether to participate in a specific conference or not. There are two different styles in Model UN: UNA-USA style and THIMUN style. The two styles have different rules and thus students who participate in a conference in one set of rule typically pursue conferences with that rule. However, because almost all conferences in Korea are UNA-USA formatted, most students tend to learn the UNA-USA method; only conferences like HAIS MUN and KIMC operate in THIMUN style out of over 30 national conferences.

There also seem to be different trends of participation in Model UN of Korea determined by the hosting organization. Students who attend international schools attend conferences hosted by international schools while students who attend foreign language high schools attend conferences hosted by universities, companies, and other students. Students who attend conferences hosted by Chosun Education usually aren't seen in other conferences as they benefit from continuous participation under Chosun Education's diverse programs. But because the awards are better in conferences hosted by universities and other companies, diverse pool of students can be seen in famous Model UN events like GC: Seoul and MUNCCC.

2.2.3. Marketing

In the early 2010s, there weren't many Model UN conferences and thus when a conference was held, it was relatively easy to gather

300~500 students. GLIS MUN gathered about 300 students in its first conference in 2010 and MUNCCC gathered over 400~500 students in its first conference in 2011 [1]. However, as more conferences were held after 2013, it came to be considered a success in 2015 if a conference had over 100 participants. Some conferences even had deficits of thousands of USD by not having enough participants. Thus to counter this problem, various Model UN conference secretariats came up with solutions to promote their conference in order to gather more participants. And here this research will explore some marketing strategies used by Model UN conferences in Korea.

SIGMUN, a conference with about 120 participants, had about 10,000 USD deficits in its first conference. However from its second conference, it had sponsors from a university in Korea, United Nations Development Program Seoul Policy Centre, a company called GTRO, and Georgetown University. And by having concrete sponsors to support SIGMUN, it was able to gain credibility among participants and was able to attract lots of participants. Also by having sponsors, the conference was even able to save fees required for borrowing conference rooms and had about 3,000 USD profits.

Although MUNCCC does not attract 400~500 participants as it did in its early days, 200~300 students still participate in this conference annually; MUNCCC does this by having attractive awards. Unlike regular Model UN conferences that have Best Delegate, Outstanding Delegate, and Honorable Mention awards, MUNCCC have ministry awards, company president awards, university president award, and etc. KIMC also had these attractions in its 2013 conference. There were three premium awards in KIMC that gave awardees 1,000 USD, 500 USD, and a full scholarship for attending a leadership camp held in an Australian university that included the flight fees.

Having awards and concrete sponsors are great; but a conference would need proper advertisements for students to get to know of its existence. Thus most conferences in Korea worked to get in touch with prospective participants by running Facebook pages and Kakao Talk groups. In Facebook pages, conferences like HAIS MUN for instance had gift prizes for those who shared HAIS MUN's advertisement. Some secretariats tried to show how the conference was being organized by uploading pictures of chair training, the venue of the conference, and etc. In order to attract participants to the conference, secretariats also advertised delegate services such as the after-conference-hotel-registration for delegates living far away from the conference venue. To have a professional ambience, many conferences also bought public domains in the internet to operate a website.

But despite these efforts, some students still couldn't participate since most conferences were at least 2 days long and students had to pay 200~400 USD in order to pay the conference fees. Therefore starting from 2013, some conferences started to eliminate Model UN's 'prestigious atmosphere' to focus on reducing the cost. CAMUN, a conference held in a local area in Korea, and HAIS MUN held in Seoul can be examples of this phenomenon. Although CAMUN was a 2~3 day conference, it eliminated expensive hotel venues and conference rooms and thus was able to reduce the participation fee to be less than 150 USD including all costs on food, hotel, and venue. The first CAMUN in 2013 succeeded with over 100 participants. HAIS MUN on the other hand reduced the conference days to one day in order to attract students who are willing to reduce both time and money spent on an event. As HAIS MUN lasted for only one day, participating students only needed to pay 50 USD. In its third conference in 2015, HAIS MUN had over 200 participants; a large success considering the fact that it was organized by high school students and that there were so many other conferences available for the participants to choose from.

Finally, it would be worth noting that several local conferences also changed its official language from English to Korean in order to make conferences more accessible to students living in the local areas who aren't very fluent in English.

3. Challenges and Prospects in 2015

3.1. Issues with Model UN Organizations

After KIMC High School Union was organized in 2011, various Model UN organizations were made. Some of those include Global Talent Raising Operation (GTRO), Model UN Association of Korea (MUNAK), and etc. For background information, GTRO is a non-profit company that is located in the southern area of Korea that helps sponsor new-found Model UN conferences; it has sponsored over 10 conferences since 2013. MUNAK on the other hand usually works in Seoul to generate a platform for discussion of Model UN society in Korea. It has the largest online Model UN platform with over 1,400 members and aims to facilitate interaction between Model UN secretariats and provide Model UN information to the public; figure 1 in this research is one of the information made by MUNAK. Most recently, a Facebook page that advertises Korean Model UN conferences was made and reached over 2,000 likes.

However despite the expansion of Model UN in Korea through various organizations, it has been difficult to maintain one. While a student may make a Model UN organization and operate it for several years, if that student grows up and moves on to the college circuit or into the job market, that student would no longer spend his/her time doing the necessary job to run that organization. Organizations like Model UN Workshops, Association of Korea Youth for Diplomacy (AKYD), and others ceased to exist from this issue.

Thus there would need to be a central force like UNA-USA in the US or WFUNA in the UN to help aid Model UN organizations founded by students to benefit the Model UN society continuously. But currently UNA-ROK in Korea only works with the college circuit to make NMUN-Korea and WFUNA simply organizes a Model UN camp annually.

3.2. Issues with Model UN Conferences

Model UN in Korea has definitely expanded. However nowadays it seems that it is too overcrowded. While it is good to have new conferences, students without much experience (3~4 conference experiences) became Secretary Generals in some conferences. Unlike the past when participants were genuinely active, nowadays only 30~40 percent of participants are active in a committee. With too many conferences and too many participants, it seems that the overall quality of Korea's Model UN has degraded to some extent.

Though there may be other reasons why students are making new conferences, it is assumed that they are essentially doing so since it would look great on their college applications. But as Model UN has become too common in college applications, it is starting to lose its merit during the admissions procedure and students looking solely for admissions benefit are exiting from the Model UN society. With its peak in 2014~15, Model UN expansion in Korea is expected to decrease. Some conferences having deficits can be an example of this phenomenon. Even the famous GLIS MUN had a deficit in its 10th conferences and changed its venue from a hotel to a university for the first time in its history in its 11th conference.

4. Conclusion

This research analyzed various aspects of Korea's Model UN society. As there hadn't been any previous research conducted in this field, this study was largely based on the author's 4 years of empirical research in the field. The development of Korea's Model UN society before 2010 was described based on the fragmented sources found in conference web pages.

Model UN is an excellent education tool to teach students the diplomatic procedures of the UN and current international issues as well as communicative competence. Students participating in Model UN can learn to perform academic research and practice public speaking. Also, if a student works as a secretariat in a conference, that student would learn vital skills needed to organize an activity.

Thus, teachers may utilize this research to exploit the educational values of Model UN. They may help students understand how Korea's Model UN works and the means to participate in it fully. Since this research analyzes how one student activity, called Model UN, has developed over decades in a nation, researchers may also utilize it to compare it with other activities for further study.

5. References

[1] Ahn, G. (2014, October 28). [Approaching Interview 15] 'GLIS'. Retrieved from http://blog.appcenter.kr./2014/1 0/glismun-glis/. Access Date: July 10, 2015.

[2] Jeung, J. Korea International Model Congress (KIMC). Retrieved from http://cafe.naver.com/hikimc. Access Date: July 6, 2015.

[3] Johnson, D.W. and Johnson, R.T. "Unleash the Power of Cooperative Learning." The School Administrator. March 1988.

[4] KICMUN Secretariat. Retrieved from http://www.kicmun.org/. Access Date: July 13, 2015.

[5] Muldoon, James, P. "The Model United Nations Revisited." *Simulation and Gaming.* March 1995.

[6] Shin, S. (2007, May 15). Youth English Debate 'Ban-Ki moon Effect'. Retrieved from http://news.donga.com/3/ all/20070515/8441800/1. Access Date: July 8, 2015.

[7] United Nations Association of Republic of Korea. Retrieved from http://www.unarok.org/main/index.php. Access Date: July 10, 2015.

[8] Welcome to HIMUN! Hankuk University of Foreign Studies International Model United Nations (HIMUN). Retrieved from http://www.himun.org/. Access Date: July 10, 2015.

7.7. Author's Model UN Resume

John Sang-Yup Lee 2012~2015

Area	Name	Year	Accolade/Position
PRESS	▸ YMS	2012	(Press)
OBSERVER	▸ HIMUN Plenary Session	2013	(Observer)
CAMPER	▸ Best Delegate Institute UCLA Summer Program	2013	Diplomacy Award
STAFF	▸ HAIS MUN	2015	(Staff)
DELEGATE	▸ HAFS MIMUN	2012	N/A
	▸ KIMC	2012	Best Delegate Award
	▸ GLIS MUN	2013	Best Delegate Award
	▸ Canada International MUN	2013	N/A
	▸ KMUN (Korea)	2013	N/A
	▸ MUNCCC	2013	YTN President Award
	▸ KIMC	2013	Melbourne University Top Conference Delegate Award
	▸ GC: Seoul	2014	Best Delegate Award
	▸ GC: International	2014	Honorable Mention Award
	▸ SIGMUN the LEGEND	2014	Georgetown University Award
CHAIR	▸ KMUN (Korea)	2014	(Crisis Chair)
	▸ Harvard World MUN	2015	(Assistant Chair)
SECRETARIAT	▸ CAMUN	2013	(Secretariat)
	▸ SIGMUN the WINTER	2014	(Advisor)
	▸ SIGMUN the THIRD	2015	(Secretariat)
	▸ MUNNEO	2015	(Advisor)

Area	Name	Year	Accolade/Position
ORGANIZATION	▸ Global Talent Raising Operation (GTRO)	2013 ~	(Co-Founder: Executive Board member)
	▸ Model UN Association of Korea (MUNAK)	2014 ~	(Co-Founder: Secretariat)
	▸ KIMC High School Union	2014 ~	(Representative of Global Vision Christian School)
PUBLICATION	▸ Model UN: Unexpected Journey	2015	Author ISBN: 978-89-6817-311-0
	▸ Exploring Model UN in Korea: Its History and Developments	2015	Author, ISBN: 978-1-908320-55-1

Epilogue

I started writing this book without intending to write it in the form a book. I initially started this writing as a booklet to give information to students at my school's Model UN club. But as the content lengthened, I thought about sharing the experience I had in Korea's Model UN society with everyone and decided to publish this as a book. I've contemplated from time to time whether I should publish this since it will be biased by my experiences. No one had previously researched and documented Korea's high school Model UN circuit and thus the book had to be mostly based on my four years of experience. Therefore, I tried my best to experience almost every parts of Korea's high school Model UN circuit to write this.

Through this book, I wanted to share information which would be hard to attain without having in-depth experience in Korea's Model UN society. Furthermore, I wanted to focus on writing a book that could draw the reader a general picture of how Model UN works in Korea so that the readers would be able to better absorb their Model UN experiences when actually participating in one. Therefore although the book contains information about the Rules of Procedures, it is dealt as one of the many aspects that constitute Model UN. I've also tried to have contents that differ from the already published books in Korea so that the information will not overlap with previous Model UN publications. I hope that you have gained some valuable information.

For four years I had attended 20 Model UN conferences in Korea's high school circuit and worked in roughly three different Model UN organizations. Model UN had a huge impact in my life: it changed how I view the world and altered the way I live. But Model UN didn't just influence me; it worked as a positive influence to numerous students as you would have seen by reading Chapter 6: Journey of Model UN. I believe that it may work to change your life too. If you haven't had any Model UN experiences, Model UN may feel like some other part of the world that's not related to you. That's exactly how *I* felt when I first attempted to do Model UN. I had no teachers or friends who knew what Model UN was. But by experiencing it, I fell in love with it. You too should experience at least one conference. You will be able to find yourself 'merging' with Model UN.

I have you have gained something from this book and wish you the best of luck in entering the world of Model United Nations.

2015. 7. 30
John Sang-Yup Lee

John Sang-Yup Lee

John (Sang-Yup) has participated in over 20 Model UN conferences for the past 4 years and was deeply involved in Korea's high school Model UN society. Starting as a press member, he attended various conferences as a staff, delegate, student officer, and a secretariat. As a delegate, among the many conferences he had participated in, he notably attended the 2014 Global Classrooms International Model UN conference held in New York as a member of Korea's representative team. He also worked as an Assistant Chair in Harvard World MUN: Seoul and organized several urban and rural conferences in Korea as a secretariat.

He also worked in different Model UN organizations in Korea. In 2013 he co-founded a non-profit company called GTRO to sponsor new found Model UN conferences and worked as a vice president in Korea's largest online Model UN forum with over 1,400 members. Recently he has published a paper titled 'Exploring Model UN in Korea: Its History and Developments' in 2015 London International Conference on Education (LICE).

For more details about the author's Model UN activities, please refer to pg 288.